Praise for *The Team Selling Solution*

"Team selling is a highly effective technique for maximizing value to the customer in a complex sale. The seamless coordination of diverse resources to solve complex client problems is critical in today's global marketplace."

Mr. Robert Dutkowsky
Chairman, President, and CEO
J. D. Edwards & Company

"Practical advice for companies large and small. Steve's team selling concepts are rock-solid and sure to get results."

Chris Killoy
VP of Sales and Marketing
Smith and Wesson

"Very little has been written about team selling, and not much more needs to be written after *The Team Selling Solution*. Steve Waterhouse has provided an excellent approach for new and veteran sales teams alike."

Alan Weiss, Ph.D.
Author of *Million Dollar Consulting*

"The complexity of our business demands that many people be involved in each sale. The team selling process provides the structure that these important players need as they work together to reach their goals."

Dave Cissell
Vice Chairman
Balboa Life and Casualty

"Over the past decade or so, the power in the B2B relationship has significantly shifted to the buying organization. The supplying organizations are striving for customer loyalty and share of customer wallet. Good team selling is particularly effective when delivering increased value in a 'solution selling' model (as opposed to product selling model). Following the methods in this book will release the power of effective team selling."

Dennis L. Rediker
President and CEO
Standard Register Co.

"Team selling takes sales to the next level. To be competitive, leaders must learn to build a sales culture that fosters cooperation across all levels and divisions to sell and serve the customer. This book is an ideal 'how-to' guide to the team selling process."

Robert Youngjohns, EVP
Global Sales Operations
Sun Microsystems

"Team selling provides an opportunity for companies to use all of their talents to sell and serve their customers. This book provides the structure for implementing a cooperative sales environment that increases sales by solving our customer's problems."

Ross Braithwait
VP of Sales
VP Buildings

"This is a book that needed to be written. Steve Waterhouse shows that team selling is not just selling with more people, but a new way of applying resources to increase sales."

Steve Smith, Chief Sales Officer
President, Global Sales and Major Sales Pursuits
EDS

"Outstanding! Steve Waterhouse has shown that success in sales results from an effective process for serving the client. Team selling is that process."

Alan Henderson
CEO
RehabCare Group

"*The Team Selling Solution* contains critical skills required to sell major accounts a complex array of products and services. Companies that fail to use team selling concepts risk leaving their customers underserved and their offerings undervalued."

Richard Reese
Chairman/CEO
Iron Mountain

"Outstanding execution is what is going to define the success of using a team selling model or other approach. Steve Waterhouse has outlined a number of great thoughts and planning ideas that should improve your ability to execute more effectively and with speed."

Scott Schafer
SVP of Sales, Marketing and Services
Reynolds and Reynolds

"Today's customers demand that we bring them integrated solutions from one unified team. *The Team Selling Solution* provides the structure and skills required to mold a single customer solution out of several independent divisions."

Bob Lento
SVP of IMG Global Sales
Convergys

The Team
Selling Solution

The Team
Selling Solution
Creating and Managing
Teams That Win the
Complex Sale

Steve Waterhouse

McGraw-Hill

New York   Chicago   San Francisco   Lisbon   London
Madrid   Mexico City   Milan   New Delhi   San Juan
Seoul   Singapore   Sydney   Toronto

The *McGraw-Hill* Companies

1 2 3 4 5 6 7 8 9 0 DOC/DOC 0 9 8 7 6 5 4 3

ISBN 0-07-141097-X

Library of Congress Cataloging-in-Publication Data

Waterhouse, Steve.
    The team selling solution : creating and managing teams that win the complex sale / by Steve Waterhouse.
        p.   cm.
Includes bibliographical references and index.
    ISBN 0-07-141097-X (alk. paper)
    1. Sales management. I. Title.
    HF5438.4.W38 2003
    658.8'1—dc21

                                                    2003008696

To my father, who taught me that anything was possible.
To my wife, Gina, who helps me realize my dreams.

Contents

Acknowledgments

What you are about to read is the result of contributions from many fine professionals. Along the way, each of them has taught me something that has brought me to this point, and you should know who they are.

I am privileged to work with many of the finest sales professionals in the world. It is ironic that they come together to learn from me, when I learn so much from them. While I could never hope to mention them all, I have to especially thank the fine sales representatives and managers and support teams at IBM, Sun Microelectronics, AT&T, Guidant, RehabCare Group, Sprague Electric, Lucent Technologies, Xerox, Taconic Laboratories, Iron Mountain, Fortune Brands, Coca-Cola Bottling, and Allmerica for their contributions. They will never know how much they have given me through their questions, problem solving, and discussions. They are the extraordinary people who actually invented team selling out of necessity.

I am also blessed with a group of colleagues who constantly inspire me to strive to higher levels of performance. They have unselfishly shared their secrets of success and helped my business grow. Each also spent many hours reading this manuscript and providing candid comments that made it a better resource for you. Dave Stein, Nancy Stephens, Bob Frare, and John Caslione each deserve a special thank-you for all they have done for me.

If you are lucky enough to have a family who supports your dreams, then you know why I must thank them. My work takes me all over the world and only rarely have they had the opportunity to join me. My wife Gina, my daughter Kat, and my son Tim have been my cheering team for many years, and I could not have reached this point without them.

Finally, thanks to my writing team: Barry Neville of McGraw-Hill, who had faith in my idea, encouraged me to publish this book, and shepherded me through the publication process beautifully; Robert Cerf at the University of Southern Maine, who spent many hours researching my ideas to give you a better book; and my wife Gina, who proofed every word a dozen times. Together, this team makes me look like a professional writer!

This book is truly, and appropriately, a team effort. As you read and apply *The Team Selling Solution,* I hope you'll be part of my team by sharing your successes and struggles. I look forward to hearing from you at *ttss@waterhousegroup.com* or 1-800-575-LEARN.

                                                        Steve Waterhouse

Introduction

Team selling is one of the fastest growing styles of selling, and yet comparatively little has been written about it. Most companies who are involved in a complex sale will find the team selling techniques offered here to be invaluable.

I wrote this book with three groups in mind:

1. The sales team leaders who must build sales teams with little or no training. They will find these techniques useful even if their company has not formally adopted the team selling philosophy.

2. The CEOs and other senior managers who are responsible for their companies' sales. This book will show them how team selling can build sales, cut costs, and improve customer satisfaction.

3. The sales team members who often get overlooked. They are the ones who make it all happen, and I believe that they can do their jobs better if they understand the entire process.

Anyone involved in multiperson sales will find value in these chapters, whether they work in a large, multinational company or a small, local operation. I have tried to highlight the areas of uniqueness whenever they occur.

Terms: I used the term *customer* throughout the book to refer to the buying company. If you use another term, such as *client,* please make the substitution. I also refer to account executives, account managers, account representatives, and all other primary sales contacts as *sales representatives.* My choice of language was not to indicate a preference but simply to be universally understood.

My intent is not to dictate the only way to operate a sales force but to stimulate ideas that can improve the systems you currently have. It is my wish that each of you will build on the ideas presented in this book and make them your own.

Happy Selling!

The Power of Team Selling

Team selling is a well-planned and coordinated effort by a selling team designed to allocate resources in such a way as to satisfy the needs for a group of customer decision makers.

National Account Management Association[1]

In many companies, including maybe your own company, team selling just happens. Unfortunately, too often it happens with devastating results. Done poorly, team selling wastes resources and hinders progress. Done correctly, team selling increases sales, reduces costs, and improves customer satisfaction. Team selling happens when your sales representative calls your factory and asks the chief engineer and the senior marketing manager to fly to Saint Louis for a customer meeting. It happens when your vice president asks to be taken into an account because it "looks interesting." It happens when it shouldn't, and it doesn't happen when it should. In this book I will show you some proven methods of using team selling to dramatically increase your sales while controlling costs and increasing customer satisfaction.

I first experienced team selling over 20 years ago as a regional sales specialist for the Sprague Semiconductor (now Allegro) Company. Back then, I was responsible for getting a group of salespeople, who were fat, dumb, and happy selling our other products, to sell semiconductors too. They didn't like the idea very much, but they went through the motions. As my sales suffered, I knew that I needed to reevaluate my strategy. That's when I realized that their "going through the motions" was hurting me. They would arrange to take me on calls, but there was never any planning. I still remember presenting a new motor-driver product to a group of bored engineers in Long Island. One of the engineers finally raised his hand and told me that no one in that plant ever used motor-drivers. I was embarrassed and my credibility was shot.

"Team selling" is not the goal: the goal is *good team selling*. What you hoped you were creating when you hired people to do a job was a family that would naturally bond and do the right things at the right times without having to be asked. This book will give you a new tool to get closer to achieving your goal of happy and productive employees serving satisfied customers through a spirit of cooperation. It can happen when you add a few effective techniques to your passion for your business.

Early in my sales career, it became clear that short briefings on the 10-minute drive from the airport to the customer site were not sufficiently preparing me or my field salespeople to do the job. The simple planning process I started back then, including premeeting calls and follow-up plans, was the beginning of our team selling programs of today.

Performed correctly, team selling can help you increase sales, revenue per customer, and customer satisfaction while reducing costs, company infighting, and missed opportunities. Although it takes effort to realize the true benefits of team selling, many companies are seeing a dramatic return on their investment of time and resources. According to Neil Rackham, author of *Spin Selling* (New York: McGraw-Hill, 1988), "Today's sales force creates value for its customers—it is not just what it sells that adds value, but the way it sells that adds value."[2] While Neil has the right idea, few traditional sales forces are delivering. In my motor-driver example, imagine what would have happened if the sales rep had asked a few questions or if he had connected me with those engineers a few days before my visit. We would have easily moved from awkward and embarrassed to competent and successful. Effective team selling can be as simple as good communication and effective planning, and the result can be a serious increase in sales.

For some companies, team selling is part of their strategic account management (SAM) program. For others, it is simply a better way to sell—by having the right group of people to serve their customers. Based on interviews with Fortune 500 companies' sales executives, managers, and human resources professionals, fewer than 24 percent of companies interviewed indicated that their organizations link people decisions to known customer needs.[3] If you feel that your company is in the 76 percent of companies that need help, pay special attention to the chapters on strategies and team building.

Who Needs Team Selling?

While many companies can benefit from the basic advantages of team selling, some selling situations virtually require a team selling approach. If your company sells complex products or multiple product lines to a single customer, you will find team selling to be essential. If you sell to multiple buyers or use manufacturer's representatives in your sales process, you will also see tremendous benefits from implementing team selling in your business. A few examples are given in Figure 1-1 to help you see how team selling might help your company.

Figure 1-1
Who Needs Team Selling and Why

Who Needs Team Selling	How They Benefit
Those who sell:	
Complex products	Coordination of experts and improved communication
Multiple product lines	Increase cross-selling and customer satisfaction
Through manufacturers' representatives	More effective use of reps, coordination of resources, and management of opportunities
To multiple buyers	More effective coordination of activities
Managers who travel	Visits that are more productive
Sales that require rapid product launches	Coordination of simultaneous sales efforts
High-level sales	Ability to sell at multiple levels in one effort
Mixed teams	Improve cross-team communication
Rapid communication	Get valuable information faster
Flat corporate structures	Improve management effectiveness
Higher customer expectations	Customers appreciate coordinated effort

Selling Complex Products

If your product or service is supported by specialists of any kind, team selling will be an effective technique for your company. Many industries have long since passed the point where a single salesperson can know all that is required to represent complex products and services. While this description may make you think exclusively of the technical world of engineers, technicians, and systems analysts, this is not the case. We are now seeing bank managers teaming with insurance and investment specialists, pharmaceutical salespeople teaming with physicians and former patients, and contractors teaming with architects and suppliers. Beyond the knowledge factor, specialists bring credibility to the sale that the salesperson may never be able to establish alone. Let's face it, salespeople lose 50 IQ points in the eyes of an engineer.

Guidant Corporation, a leading developer of cardiovascular medical products, uses teams to ensure their physician customers have the best information possible to save lives. In addition to the account representative, each customer is served by a team of clinical specialists. Most of these specialists are experienced professionals previously employed in the same types of jobs as their counterparts in the customer hospitals. They are respected for their knowledge and experience. As a result, Guidant has earned the position of leader in the field and has earned the right to spend time with those who make critical buying decisions. What could be more important than that in sales?

Sales teams should also include other internal resources, ranging from accounting to customer service to executive management. As you will see, teams are designed to support both the customer's needs and the selling company's needs in a complex transaction.

Selling Multiple Product Lines

Team selling is a powerful technique if your company sells multiple product lines and wants you to increase your sales per account. In situations where each line is handled by a separate group, team selling is a way of joining forces to sell more and serve the customer in a more unified way. When a single representative is responsible for selling multiple product lines, team selling can be the framework for the coordination of information and resources from the different product groups through the sales representative and on to the customer. As Deming said in point 9 of his 14 points, "Break down barriers between departments. People in research, design, sales and production must work as a team."[4]

You can imagine the possibilities that an accounting firm can realize by breaking down such barriers. A typical firm has separate departments offering auditing, tax advice, corporate financing, and payroll. By coordinating their approach to the customer, each department can assist the other in capturing more business and providing an integrated set of services to the customer. Done correctly, everyone wins.

Using Manufacturers' Representatives

If your company sells through manufacturers' representatives, value-added resellers, or distributors, you will find team selling can be the answer to the constant tug of war between the manufacturers, the representatives, and your end customers. This process will give order to the sales effort that was dominated by forced "ride-alongs" and obligatory sales reports. It will ensure that each party is playing the appropriate role in serving the customer and expanding the market.

Selling to Multiple Buyers

Your customers have replaced clerks with educated professionals, diminishing the role of the buyer as the primary point of contact. Decisions are made by committees who are difficult to identify and harder still to contact. Many purchases have enterprise-wide implications and call for multilocation and even international points of contact. Mike Cohn, manager of Global Sales Programs for Hewlett-Packard, said, "To maintain leadership, HP must do more than provide superior products and services at competitive prices; [HP] must be the easiest and most effective company to do business with."[5]

Team selling can help you build and coordinate the many contacts that influence the buying decision. My goal in the following chapters is to show you how to incorporate these contacts in an effective process that ensures that valuable knowledge and relationships are not lost or squandered. Team selling uses a multiple-contact approach to build new relationships at all levels of your customer's organization. The result is a deeper and longer-lasting bond between you and your customer, resulting in greater sales at lower costs.

Managers Who Travel

Even if your company sells simpler products or services, team selling can be the answer to the question, "How do my managers and executives work with my representatives and customers in the field?" Done correctly, management teaming is a powerful sales tool. Done wrong, it reduces the power of the sales representative and overloads the executive with direct phone calls from the customer.

One of our rules for team selling is that managers never go into the field without a plan from the sales rep. No more mandatory account visitations for the sole purpose of checking up on the reps. Let's end the accidental activities. Each customer meeting should be part of a coordinated effort to advance particular issues and increase the probability of closing sales. Managers can, and must, add value. Team selling means planning, and we ask managers and other members of the team to demand to see a plan before any action is taken.

Rapid Product Launches

As the life cycles of your products collapse, team selling's importance as a means of shortening the sales cycle increases. The parallel sales techniques made possible by the team selling process ensures you of the maximum access to the greatest number of decision makers in the shortest time. Shorter selling cycles can mean a larger market share and higher profit margins.

Pharmaceutical companies are under the gun from the day a patent is issued. From then until it expires, they must enter the market and maximize sales before the competition moves in. The high cost of research makes this short selling cycle a high-stakes game. With HMOs and hospital buying groups concentrating the decision making in a few places, quickly penetrating these key accounts is important. No longer can these companies rely on one salesperson to work through the chain of influencers. Today, sales teams must strategize and coordinate their efforts to bring their message to the right people now!

Speed is also important in competitive situations, such as when your competition is already ahead of you on a given opportunity. Today's customers are looking for more than features and benefits; they want to work with a company that is organized and efficient, from the sales process to the final delivery. A fast and effective sales process can often derail a competitor's other advantages.

High-Level Sales

Enterprise-wide solutions require corporate-level commitments from both parties. As a result, your senior management team may be added to the sales team to serve the role of "partner-maker." Too few sales representatives or executives know how to effectively integrate their roles into an ongoing sales process. In team selling, the roles are clearly defined and proper premeeting planning is required. As a result, more sales are closed and fewer executives waste time cooling their heels in the customer's lobby.

I remember one CEO who demanded to see the president of a major computer company. He could not understand why his company did not have business with this account, and no amount of coaching by the account manager could convince him to work with his team on the sale. His pushy letter was returned to his company's sales representative with this note: "Your CEO is welcome to visit our lobby any time he wants to spend the entire day on our couch." Had he worked with his team, they might have been able to use him as an effective lever to gain access to the customer's senior management.

Fund-raising companies and nonprofit organizations like the United Way also use teams of executives to gain access to other executives and build rapport at higher levels. Done properly, these meetings can be part of a well-orchestrated sales plan, with each player serving the most appropriate role. Team selling defines these roles and provides you with a framework for the successful execution of your strategy.

Mixed Teams

Your inside sales representatives often talk with customers more frequently than their corresponding field representatives. In many companies this leads to confusion for both sales reps and the customer. The traditional "who promised what when" battle ends in frustration for all involved. Team selling provides a framework for coordinating the internal or selling-side communication and teamwork. Used properly, your inside sales representatives can free up the field force to uncover new opportunities. Increased sales and improved customer service result.

Team selling requires that each member of the team recognize that the account is owned by the company and not any individual. As such, it is in everyone's best interest to share knowledge with the entire team. Through this open sharing, the full benefit of team selling can be realized.

Rapid Communication

If you have ever sat through a production planning meeting, you know this scenario: The field has information about changing customer demand, but it is not reported to the factory until the next forecasting cycle. As a result, expensive excess inventory or market-damaging shortages disrupt the company's P&L. Much of this problem can be traced back to the fact that the salespeople and operations people are on different teams. They may speak different languages, are often rewarded for conflicting goals, and see customers from completely different points of view. Where Sales sees an opportunity to sell a cutting-edge product or service, Marketing sees only one more opportunity to add to the "demand list." Where Sales sees a potential commission and a new car, Operations sees the potential for unrecouped tooling charges that could blow their bonuses and Florida vacations.

Building teams that include all interested parties improves both communication and understanding within your selling organization. A true sales team is thinking about the good of the company and is rewarded for its ability to work together to help your company reach its goals.

Flat Corporate Structures

The flattening of many corporate structures has left a void in the field sales organization that self-managed sales teams can fill. Where GE sales managers oversaw 17 sales representatives only a few years ago, today they oversee 40.[6] Who is left to provide the feedback, coaching, motivating, and goal setting that has been a significant part of their development? A study of sales and service representatives of a regional Bell operating company may shed some light. When these workers were moved from a "directed" style of management to self-managed teams, sales increased by 9.3 percent.[7] Qualitative research suggested that the benefits were a result of group goal setting, problem solving, and learning. It is easy to see how these results could be repeated and enlarged upon in other organizations that are dealing with the same challenges.

Your sales teams, especially if they are self-managed teams, may assume many of the roles traditionally assigned to the sales manager. Given the proper training and support, these teams can provide accurate forecasts, set and achieve higher goals, provide accurate marketing feedback, and effectively train and motivate their members. Mature teams often request and manage other corporate resources and monitor expenses, and they can even be responsible for their own P&L, where appropriate.

Having worked with many of these teams as a consultant and trainer, I have found them to be more competent than even they realized. I regularly do an exercise where we post the members' problems and challenges on a wall. In the next step, the team members are asked to revisit the wall and to add their own possible solutions to any of the problems that they feel competent to comment on. The results are always eye-opening. Individuals discover 3 to 10 possible solutions to each of their problems. In addition, they usually find another team member who has triumphed over a similar situation and is willing to coach them through their challenge. My experience shows that given the proper training and encouragement, teams are more effective at problem solving than their managers.

Given these benefits, companies that have overtaxed their managers due to rapid expansion or downsizing can easily see the advantage of implementing a team selling strategy. While the effort to make the transition is significant, the payback can be enormous and long lasting.

Higher Customer Expectations

Global competition has allowed our customers to raise their expectations to the highest levels ever. Not only are your customers looking for great products, unique solutions, and competent company representatives, they now expect competent partners. Today customers may expect

- One point of contact for every product you sell

- Your divisions to work together seamlessly during the sales process and long afterward

- You to facilitate the relationship

- You to coordinate all the details

- That you will never drop the ball

- Clear, concise communications between all parties

Team selling was designed to help you address these very expectations.

I had the opportunity to work with IBM's African sales team and to meet the account representative responsible for software sales to 27 sub-Saharan countries. When I commented that she had some dangerous places to visit, she laughed. She explained that especially during wartime, her customers expected great service. "If something is damaged or destroyed, it must be replaced. That's our job." She had a unique team supporting her and each understood the unique needs of the customers in their difficult territory. Together they won business that less organized companies could never have handled. John A. Caslione, noted international expert on developing global business and author of the best-selling book *Global Manifest Destiny* (Dearborn Publishing, 2001), states that "Integrated cross-functional sales, marketing and customer service teams are absolutely essential in expanding an enterprise's ability to manage global customer relationships successfully in the new global marketplace."

If you recognize your company in any of the scenarios mentioned in this chapter, team selling may be just the tool to help your company sell more, sell faster, and create happier and more loyal customers.

Summary

Our business world has changed and continues to change at an ever-increasing rate. Tom Peters once stated, "The ability to

change and adapt is our only sustainable competitive advantage."
Team selling is the critical missing component in the evolution
of the sales process. For those who have dreams of success in
today's marketplace, now is the time to change and adapt using
team selling.

2

Don't Use a Hammer to Build Your Team

*Individual commitment to a group effort—that is what
makes a team work, a company work, a society work, a civiliza-
tion work.*

Vince Lombardi

It may sound obvious, but the first question to ask yourself in
setting up your team is "Why bother?" Teaming is complicated and takes effort, so there should be a good reason for
doing it. In my mind, sales teams are created for one reason:
to improve the odds of building an effective rapport with and
making a profitable sale to a satisfied customer. If teaming is
not likely to accomplish this goal, I recommend that you don't
use it.

Put simply, team selling is fundamental to your success in situations where you must bring one or more of the following benefits to your sales effort:

- Technical knowledge beyond that of the sales representative

- Credibility with the customer's specialists

- Customer specific knowledge or history

- Industry specific insights

- Additional resources to handle varied tasks

- More eyes and ears on the account

- Representatives who can sell other product lines

- Operations or factory representatives

- Senior managers who can make larger commitments

- Representatives who cover other customer facilities

- Improved internal and external communications

> Use teams when they will improve your ability to sell and serve your customer or to do either of these tasks faster.

In short, if more knowledge, more resources, or more speed will make the difference in the sale, team selling is your tool. In most cases, your team will be developed to deliver several of the benefits mentioned above. Even if you have a two-person team, the right team structure can make the difference between success and failure. Incorporate these desired benefits into your team goals and structure.

Types of Teams

You must customize your team's selling process to fit a wide range of business needs. For this reason, the types of teams used should be varied, and the teams should be flexible to fit your situation. I have defined four basic configurations of teams to help you structure one that is best suited for your needs.

Teams can be *static* or *dynamic,* referring to the permanency of the members, and *horizontal or vertical,* depending on whether the members come from a single department or many departments.

Static Teams for Consistency

Static teams tend to be fixed in composition and assigned to one account or project. Major account teams often fall into this category, as do teams created to work on a specific long-term opportunity or project. The benefits of static teams include the development of an effective working relationship among team members and the reduction of "turnover time" as new members join the team. Over time, the static teams can also develop a deep and effective rapport with the customer.

Examples of static teams can be found in cities like New York where companies open sales offices specifically to sell to the major companies headquartered there. These teams are often dedicated to one account and can remain together for years.

Another example is that of a company that uses a static team to serve an account that buys custom machine parts for military applications. The team is highly skilled and has worked on the project for years. The complexity of the military specifications makes it difficult to move team members in and out of the project on a frequent basis.

One of the primary disadvantages is that static teams can get stale and may exist long after their need has passed, thus increasing their costs. We all know the stories of the old sales manager who has been there for years and "knows it all." In a fast-changing world, know-it-alls are often clueless. To cure this, put a review date

> Static teams can help in complex sales and long-term relationships.

on all teams so you can evaluate their effectiveness and value. Make it a policy to rotate a percentage of the team on an annual basis to keep fresh ideas moving in and to terminate the team when the need has passed.

Advantages of static teams:

- They can build mature relationships.

- They can develop deep customer knowledge.

- They have time to earn the customer's trust.

Disadvantages of static teams:

- The lack of change can make them stale.

- They can be expensive to staff.

Dynamic Teams for Flexibility

Dynamic teams change members as needed and are created and disbanded as your needs come and go. They are created to achieve a specific purpose such as selling a major contract or supporting a large sales presentation. Since your dynamic teams are created around projects, there tend to be many more of them at any given time. Dynamic teams can be established quickly and informally to address a specific need or maintained over the lifetime of a project with new members added as needed.

If your company sells enterprise-wide solutions, dynamic teams may already be at work in your company. The sales representative probably built the first one to meet with the customer and identify their needs. The team was changed slightly to present your proposal and changed again after the contract was won to begin the implementation. While there was a common theme and goal to all of these groups, the specific resources required changed with the evolving need.

Dynamic teams can be as small as two people. Years ago I was buying a new copier for a newspaper my wife and I owned. This was before the days of scanners and extensive computer graphics, so the copier was going to be used to enlarge simple graphics and drawings to use in our customers' ads. The first three copier sales teams that came to my office knew nothing about my application and totally missed my needs in their presentation. Finally, the Mita Copier team arrived with an account representative and a technician who happened to be in the area. The salesperson was well-dressed and polite, but after a little discussion, it was clear that he did not understand our business or how we used his products.

Eventually, the technician, whose hands were stained with black toner, spoke up. He had fixed the copiers at several area advertising agencies where they did ad layout similar to ours. The quiet-spoken technician understood the unique nature of our needs and recommended the best machine for the job. From then on, the salesperson always brought that technician with him when it was time for me to buy a new copier. The combination of technical knowledge, industry specific insights, and credibility made the technician perfectly suited for this dynamic team.

On the downside, dynamic teams are often forced to get up to speed so quickly that they miss the important bonding stages that can improve team structure and outcomes. To remedy this, schedule time early in their formation for the entire team to meet face-to-face. Include enough group social time for the members to get to know each other. One night on the town can return years of benefits. Even teleconferences can help build the team.

> A good team is measured by the value that each member brings to the effort.

Advantages of dynamic teams:

- Rapid change gives them flexibility.

- Since they can be created instantly, they can respond to the need quickly.

- They are focused on one issue.

Disadvantages of dynamic teams:

- Lack of team-building time can cause a weak team structure.

- There may be poor continuity due to changing members.

- Constant training is required as new members are added.

Horizontal Teams for Breadth

Many major corporations acquire companies to add product lines to their offerings. Their goals are to capture a greater percentage of a customer's business and develop a relationship with the customer across many divisions. Unfortunately, the natural divisions or functional "silos" prevent this from happening. Horizontal teams may be the answer.

Horizontal teams are composed of representatives of several divisions within your company. The goal is to coordinate the sale of multiple product lines through separate selling groups.

Sun Microsystems is an example of a company that uses horizontal teams. They have divisions that sell servers, consulting, software, and Internet services independently. When they are selling to a major account, they form a horizontal sales team to coordinate their service to the customer. In this way, the divisions can remain autonomous while the customer receives a coordinated suite of products and services. This team also helps Sun share information between groups that aids the other groups in positioning their offerings.

A manufacturer's rep company uses horizontal teams to sell their multiple product lines. They remain the primary contact while serving the customer with representatives from 20 or 30 different suppliers.

Horizontal teams can be a cost-effective alternative to reengineering your company since they allow each division to remain

focused on its own specialty, while the customer sees a broad
and unified product offering.

On the downside, hori-
zontal teams can be difficult to
manage since the members
owe allegiance to different
departments and bosses. This

> Horizontal teams coordinate
> multiple offerings within a
> single group.

can also increase the time required to coordinate meetings
and other activities. These issues can be addressed by ensuring
that there is adequate support and commitment from senior
management.

Advantages of horizontal teams:

- Increases cross-selling opportunities

- Allows divisions to remain focused

- Improves customer support

Disadvantages of horizontal teams:

- Difficult to manage across multiple departments

- Split loyalty

- Takes time to coordinate

Vertical Teams for Depth

Vertical teams bring together resources from many sources
within your company to sell and serve your customer on a specific

opportunity. Unlike the horizontal teams, the goal here is to sell one specific product or service. It is not uncommon for the team to include the full range of positions from senior vice president to junior technician. Vertical teams support sales representatives on given opportunities or key accounts. They can be created on-the-fly by the account repre-sentative to meet a customer opportunity or developed over time to manage a specific large project.

> Vertical teams allow a complex sale to be handled in an organized process.

Companies such as General Electric use vertical teams to sell expensive medical imaging equipment to hospitals. To sell one piece of equipment, the team may include a sales repre-sentative, a lab technician, a maintenance specialist, a medical professional, a financial analyst, and a member of senior man-agement. With state governments regulating the installation of new hospital facilities, many teams even include a lobbyist and a lawyer.

One food processing company in the Midwest has used vertical teams to sell custom-branded frozen meals to grocery store chains. The team includes a chef to develop the recipe, a graphic artist to design the packaging, a logistics expert to handle shipping, and the sales representative to pull it all together.

As you can see, the value of a vertical team increases with the complexity of the sale. This can be the result of many factors, including a complex product, difficult delivery process, and unique application.

On the negative side, vertical teams add cost and manage-ment overhead to the sales process. Both can be minimized through proper team management and should be included in the goals and mission of the team.

Advantages of vertical teams:

- Highly focused on single opportunity

- Responsive to customer needs

- Easily assembled by a single representative

Disadvantages of vertical teams:

- Can be expensive due to increased travel and resources

- Difficult to manage compared with a single sales representative

As you may have realized, the team configurations defined in this section are not mutually exclusive. Both horizontal and vertical teams can be created as static or dynamic teams. The definitions are provided as a way of developing a common language that we can use as we define the teaming needs of a given situation.

Other descriptions are also helpful in understanding the makeup of sales teams. We will discuss several in Chapter 3.

Matching the Team to the Customer

Sales teams are often built to work with a specific opportunity or customer. When building a customer-focused team, remember that the goal is to make the customer happy with your products, services, and ability to deliver. Using the information you gather in your investigative phase, you must build a team that addresses

Figure 2-1
Match Your Team to the Customer

Name	Knowledge	Relationships	Geography	Availability	Credibility	Strategy	Match-up	Motivation

Rate each team member by what they bring to the team:
1 = high, 2 = average, 3 = low

as many of the customer's needs as possible. As more information is gathered, change the team to ensure continued customer focus.

As you pick your team, attempt to cover as many of the following areas as possible (Figure 2-1):

- *Knowledge*—of product, customer, and team

- *Relationships*—with customer and team

- *Geography*—close to the action

- *Availability*—free from other commitments

- *Credibility*—recognized expert

- *Strategy*—gives you an advantage

- *Match-up*—had a counterpart on the customer's team

- *Motivation*—a desire to help

Knowledge.   Do you have members who know the customer, product, industry, application, and individuals at the customer? Is their information current and complete enough for this project? Are there questions you hope the customer won't ask you? If so, whom should you get to handle them? Gone are the days of "investigative" sales calls, where you asked 20 questions to learn about the company. The Internet has made research simple and basic knowledge a prerequisite. If you do not have a "knowledge specialist" in your company to add to your team, create the position for one. Assign team members research tasks and build a file on the customer. If possible, share this information on your intranet with others in your company who could benefit from it. Knowledge itself is not power, but the application of it certainly can be powerful.

Relationships.   Do you have team members who already have relationships with critical members of the customer's team? Do you have team members who can quickly build and maintain relationships where you need them?

A trucking company I was working with had built a list of target accounts that included Coca-Cola. In a training session, the Atlanta rep admitted that he did not know anyone at Coke and was going into the account cold. There were 40 other sales reps in the room from around the country, so I asked if any of them had good contacts at Coke. We uncovered two who had good contacts at other Coke plants and one who had worked with the Atlanta buyer when he worked for another company. These contacts were invaluable in helping the Atlanta rep sell the account and showed the entire group the value of working together.

Geography.　Do you have members who are located near the customer's various sites and can maintain a physical presence there? Yes, I know you can fly there on a day's notice, but that's not the point. Having a person on the ground and able to meet with the customer on a moment's notice can give you a significant advantage. We all know that we are more likely to build a rapport with someone we can see in person than someone we meet over the phone. The higher the frequency of face-to-face meetings, the greater are your chances of building an effective rapport with each customer contact.

Availability.　Do you have access to internal resources that will be available when you need them in order to avoid rescheduling customer meetings? There is a tendency for us to choose the best people to join our team. Sounds logical, doesn't it? But how about this: The best people are always busy, and you'll never get them to the customer site or team meetings when you need them. As an alternative, try choosing a more available resource and leave your top dog for emergencies. A committed group of "B players" can often outsell a distracted group of "A players."

Credibility.　Do you have members who will be credible in customer meetings? Your assessment of the customer's team will tell you who you are up against. Some people just like to show how much they know by attacking your support team. Others are quite happy with an occasional "I don't know." This is one area where you may need to make adjustments as you learn more about the account.

Credibility can be very personal. I had a Ph.D. scientist on a team who made very few points with most buyers and executives. They saw him as aloof and disinterested. On the other hand, the quality assurance engineers couldn't get enough of him. They hung on his every word and constantly called him for advice. Recognize the individual pairing in your team and ensure that you have credible matches where they count.

Strategy. Do you have the required team members to execute your sales strategy with this account? In Chapter 9 we discuss strategies in depth, but for now let's assume you have a plan for selling this account from a variety of angles. You must be prepared with the resources that your plan requires. When reality strikes and your team gets cut, don't spread your team players too thin. Rework your plan and execute to the best of your ability with the resources you have.

Match-up. Do you have members to match up with every member of the customer's buying team? At a minimum, your team must reflect the composition of the customer's buying team. If they include engineers and scientists, you'll need engineers and scientists. If they have a senior VP, you'll eventually need a senior VP. Remember, the brightest sales representative may be discounted by the dumbest scientist, and title trumps everything (or at least in the mind of the person with the title it does!).

Earlier I stated that a one-to-one match-up was the minimum because you may decide go beyond the customer's defined group. If your sales strategy has identified other influencers who are not included in the customer-defined process, it might be to your advantage to bring them in. We'll discuss this in more detail in the strategy section of Chapter 9.

It is important to note here that I am not recommending that you build big teams for the sake of size. Having more players does not win the day. Having the *right* players does. You will find that many of your team members can serve several of the roles defined above. We are not trying to overwhelm the customer, we are just trying to be prepared to answer questions and move the sale forward.

Motivation.   You know how tough it is to build a team even when your people want to do the job. It is nearly impossible when they don't. Several years ago, a company that serviced nuclear power plants called me to train their technical staff. The company had just laid off all of their site managers in a budget-cutting move, and they had a great idea to fill the gap with technical staff. The site managers had been responsible for attending customer lunches and dinners and other important occasions and both companies felt that these informal gatherings were important to their relationship. Now that the site managers were gone,

> Fill your team like you fill a tool belt: Add people you will need to perform the various tasks in your sales process.

my job was to teach the techies to schmooze. As an engineer myself, I knew that the last place these people wanted to be was at a company luncheon, holding a drink in one hand, a soggy paper plate in the other, and somehow trying to shake hands.

As you can imagine, it was a disaster, and we had a very unmotivated group to work with. The obvious point is: Pick motivated people for your team or find out what will motivate them.

Build a Team, Not a Gang!

When you dump a group of people together in a room, you have a gang, not a team. A gang is a group of people with some common interest but without the skills to work together effectively. Teams require training to learn to function effectively. Without this training, you might be better off not teaming in the first place.

One major catalog company decided to use teams to sell a new branded credit card. They picked the best people and told them what the plan was. Unfortunately, they cut the budget for training and never showed them how to work together to achieve their goals. As a result, they not only failed to reach their quota on credit card sales, but several experienced people left the company out of frustration. It was a major loss on all counts.

Fortunately, there is a relatively predictable set of four steps that most teams progress through on their way to effectiveness: organize, define, strategize, and perform.

Steps to Building an Effective Team

Organize.   During this phase, the team is coming together and getting to know one another. They will set goals, make preliminary plans, and generate ideas about the tasks in front of them. This is the time to define initial roles and ensure that everyone is included in the activities.

> *Tasks to build the team:* Casual social opportunities are important to generate interaction.
> *Problems to identify:* Watch for loners or anyone who is not participating or who is excluded from the team.

Define.   Now that they know one another, they can get down to work. In this phase the team can define the job ahead of them and select the issues to be addressed. Lists of problems are developed and addressed.

> *Tasks to build the team:* Address issues of status and rank. Clarify roles and share expertise.
> *Problems to identify:* Watch for power struggles and rank issues.

Strategize.   At this stage the team can deal with the heavier issues of strategy and resource allocation. They will address rank issues and compensation. Boundaries will be established and rules of communication will be agreed on.

> *Tasks to build the team:* Address power differences and interpersonal problems. Make the team aware of the benefits of other opinions and approaches to solving problems. Help them deal with territorial issues.
> *Problems to identify:* Look for unequal participation and ineffective communications.

Perform.   The team is performing tasks at this stage and dealing with real issues.

> Training is the oil that makes teams work smoothly.

> *Tasks to build the team:* Work on communications and presentations issues. Help them execute their strategy.
> *Problems to identify:* Watch for the team to run into the limits of their team training and begin in-fighting or sabotage.

Defining Responsibility for Tasks

Each time a task is assigned, responsibility goes with it. Over the years, I have learned that there is one person who never gets anything done. That person is "somebody," as in "somebody needs to feed the dog" or "somebody needs to mow the lawn." Listen for the somebodies in your meetings and assign them away. The three types of assignments possible for any task are accountability, support, and resource.

> *Accountability:* This person is responsible for the completion of the task, no excuses.
>
> *Support:* This person has pledged time to help the accountable person in the completion of the task, but he or she is not responsible for its completion.
>
> *Resource:* A person who has information that may be useful to those working on the task. The person has not committed to working on the task, only to answering some questions or pointing the way to the answers.

If you want to avoid hours of arguments over missed deadlines, follow this simple rule: Define the accountable person at the same time that a task is assigned. I also strongly recommend that support and resources also be defined at the same time. Done correctly, this ends the blame game, increases peer pressure, and improves the probable outcome of the assignment.

> Never leave critical tasks unassigned.

Summary

A team is not simply a group of people who want to get something done. A team is a group of the right people with the right skills who know how to work together to accomplish a complex task. If you design your teams correctly, you will maximize your chances of success.

3

Everyone Has a Role
to Play

*Never doubt that a small, committed group of people can
change the world. Indeed, it is the only thing that ever has.*

Margaret Mead

Both the power and the complexity of a team increase expo-
nentially with the number of team members. Each additional
person adds new opportunities to connect with customers and
the potential for conflicts and missed communication with
other team members. To reduce the downside and maximize
the benefits to be gained from the addition of each new team
member, clearly define the roles and responsibilities before
bringing new members to the team.

You will note that the role descriptions that follow are not detailed and rigid. I firmly believe that smart people can work out the details when given the structure or outline. This chapter is intended to help you as you guide your teams to an effective structure.

You will also notice that I do not mention the sales process in this chapter. It is discussed in Chapter 7. My goal is to make team selling as universal as possible through the development of roles that can overlay any defined process. You will, however, find that team selling works much better if your company has an agreed-upon sales process that is being actively used in the field. The process provides one additional important guideline for the team to follow.

Roles and Responsibilities

When teams get out of control and quickly became dysfunctional, the problem may be the lack of definitions of roles and responsibilities. Unfortunately, the correct makeup of the team may not be obvious from the beginning. It often takes time and experience with the customer to determine the best blend of resources for a given sale. As the teams get larger and more diverse, the need for clear roles and responsibilities becomes even greater.

Rather than define the roles by traditional job titles, our firm has found it more effective to define the work by the required tasks and then let the appropriate team members step into the various roles as needed.

| Focus on roles not titles. |

This process accomplishes two goals. First, it allows the job of team organizing to be free of the constraints of job titles and ranks. Second, it allows the flexibility that is required as customers' needs change and problems occur.

For ease of discussion, let's separate the roles into major and minor categories. This is done not to define their importance but to identify those that appear in most teams versus those that tend to be more application specific.

Major Roles

The major roles include the owner, the scout, the progress manager, the specialist, the power player, and the approver. You will find that teams of 2 or 20 will have all of these roles on the team. In smaller teams, one person will play many roles. In most cases, the roles will move from person to person as the sale progresses.

The Owner

The owner is the one person who is ultimately responsible for the success of the account. This is usually the account representative who initially approached the account. This role will often be moved to a major account specialist if the account reaches a sufficient size. In many organizations, the power to make major decisions or commit significant resources rests with this person.

In companies with fully executed self-managed teams, the owner's role can actually be held by the team itself. If a point person is required for reporting purposes, the team will assign one.

The owner is usually the person who your customer sees as their top contact. The owner facilitates most major customer meetings and handles serious issues. One of my clients has used the owner concept very effectively. They sell supplies to research laboratories and their account representatives have technical backgrounds and are competent to handle most situations.

Recently, the company has been in the acquisition mode and has brought in several new lines. The account representative must now bring in other specialists and move out of the direct selling role. As she does, she still maintains account control as the owner and the one who sees the big picture.

> The owner is the one person who is ultimately responsible for the account.

Companies selling to multiple locations may assign an owner for each site and one for the overall account. This keeps the accountability clear to ensure that someone is paying attention to the results at each level.

One major problem in implementing team selling strategies is integrating the role of the owner into the team. Some fiercely independent salespeople may resent the team involvement, while the teams can feel steamrolled by a directive-style salesperson. I will address this point several times in later chapters.

Skills required of the owner:

- The ability to move comfortably and quickly from a solo role to a team role since they will find themselves in this position quite often

- The ability to manage through influence rather than power

- The ability to maintain relationships with the broadest range of people

The Scout

I love this job! The scout is responsible for finding the opportunities and identifying the initial points of contact. Scouts may also research and qualify the opportunity before bringing it to the team. Since the salesperson is usually the first person on the scene, he serves as the scout for the initial stages of the sale. As the sale develops, it is possible that the best scouts will be the technical specialists who are brought in to work deep in the customer's operations.

My favorite role when I sold semiconductors was that of the scout. I made it a point to get a plant tour, even if it was the last step in getting shown to the door by the buyer (not that I was thrown out too often!). By seeing the products the customer was building, I could usually identify two or three opportunities where our products would offer the customer considerable savings.

Never underestimate the power of the other team members to serve as effective scouts. As I was touring a plant with a marketing manager, he noticed that the infusion pump that this company manufactured did not have a tamper-proof door latch. He was aware that this

> Scouts can be anyone on the team who actively seeks out opportunities to sell.

was a pending regulation and suggested a solution to the buyer, who immediately called the senior engineer, and we made the sale.

In a telecommunications company in Pennsylvania, the scouts are the customer service representatives who talk to customers with problems. They are trained to ask questions and find opportunities to expand their offerings to the customer.

Effective scouting requires training. In a multiproduct horizontal team, each product group should teach the other team members how to identify opportunities for their product or service. In an insurance sales team, the life insurance specialist might tell the team to look for employees who are critical to the success of the company. Firms often insure the life of these people with what is called *key man insurance.* Scouts do not

need to be experts in every field to be effective. They simply need
to know what indicators to look for or what questions to ask.

Skills required of the scout:

- The ability to penetrate new accounts or divisions of
  accounts

- The ability to determine if opportunities exist

- The ability to overcome many types of sales resistance

- The ability to build networks of supporters who will
  lead the scout through the corporate maze to the real
  decision makers

- A working knowledge of the product or service and its
  applications

- An understanding of the customer's business and the
  industry in which they operate

- The ability to research corporate and industry trends
  and to analyze their effect on the customer's current
  situation

- The ability to move comfortably from a solo position
  to a team position

The Progress Manager

This is a role that will be new to many of you, even though
most of you have done it. The progress manager makes it all
move forward. Large sales are more like projects than events. As

such, they need a manager to oversee the list of tasks, deadlines, and commitments. The progress managers are responsible for checking on the various team members to ensure that everything that should be done is being done. If balls are dropped, the progress manager reassigns those tasks to ensure a successful sale.

Progress managers also arrange team and customer meetings and follow up with key customer contacts. In the early stage of a sale, the owner and the progress manager roles are both taken by the account representative. Later, as the complexity of these tasks expands, you may split one or both of these roles off to allow the account representative to return to scouting new opportunities.

If you have been a major account manager, you have often found yourself in the role of progress manager since you are the one with the account-wide focus. It is important that this role be assigned and not assumed, since a single major account may have literally hundreds of opportunities in process simultaneously. One example is a robotics company whose major accounts include the big-three car companies. The team includes account representatives in the field who call on the individual plants and a major account manager in Detroit with company-wide responsibility. Their practice is to keep the progress manager role at the account rep level until multiple plants are involved. At that point the

> The progress manager is responsible for moving the sale forward.

progress manager responsibility is formally handed to an inside sales rep who coordinates activities. This frees up the account reps to scout for new opportunities and increase their sales. It is a win-win for everyone involved.

You can see the progress manager role at work in the sale of retail clothing. The complex buying process must be managed from the runway to the rack. The progress manager role moves accordingly from the sales representative to the operations manager. The key is to keep this time-intensive role in the hands of the person who can do the most good and away from those who should be focusing on other priorities.

Skills required of the progress manager:

- They must be organized!

- Many use project management software to develop Gantt and PERT charts of the sales plan.

- They must be effective communicators and effective managers.

- They need to be effective motivators because they manage without power since few of the team members actually report to them.

- For large teams, meeting management and video conferencing are critical skills.

The Specialist

Specialists come in many varieties, the most common being the technical expert. Specialists bring three important, highly interlinked benefits to the selling team. They have (1) knowledge, (2) credibility, and (3) peer rapport.

Knowledge. Specialists bring knowledge that the other members of the team lack and could not easily acquire. It is hard to think of something that has not gotten complex enough to justify a specialist. Pitney Bowes is an example of a company that has made effective use of specialists in their sales teams. As field salespeople gain experience, they are trained to become specialists on specific machines in the Pitney Bowes line. As a result, when a salesperson selling postage meters identifies an opportunity for a copier sale, he will team with a trained copier specialist to make the customer presentation.

Industry specialists can also be valuable to a team. Industry experts speak the customer's language and understand their unique needs. Software companies selling enterprise-wide accounting packages often use industry experts to assist in the sale. They give their customer a feeling that their needs will be addressed correctly. Outside consultants often serve as industry specialists in these situations.

Company specialists are people from within the selling organization who have unique knowledge of the history and workings of the customer's organization. These may be strategic account managers or just employees with many years on the account. They can serve a valuable role in developing your sales strategy or even help with introductions to key players.

Credibility. Specialists also bring credibility to the team. Unfortunately, salespeople often lose points in the credibility department by the very nature of their job. For this reason, even a very knowledgeable salesperson will add a specialist to the team, especially when meeting with the customer's specialists.

In a small machine tool company in Chicago, the specialist is actually the CEO. He designed the unique tools that the company produces and is respected by the customers for his knowledge of their problems. He brings enormous credibility with him.

A unique type of specialist is found in companies doing joint-marketing efforts. In these situations, a specialist from one company may accompany the sales team from another. This situation requires sensitivity and trust and, for that reason, is a high-risk scenario. To complicate matters, it is often the account representative from company B that accompanies the selling team from company A. This complicates roles further and compounds the risk of conflict and failure. I address this further in Chapter 11.

Rapport.   Never underestimate the value of the rapport that specialists can build with their peers in the customer company. Specialists and their counterparts will often discuss details of the deal that would never be disclosed by the buyer or senior managers. Since specialists are not seen as salespeople, their counterparts are less guarded around them. A medical specialist for one of my customers told me that it feels like he is invisible to the customer. When he is alone with the customer's specialists, they discuss the sales team, the deal, and the competition openly in front

> Specialists can improve customer contacts through their unique abilities.

of him. It always amazes him that they seem to ignore the fact that he might take the information back to his team.

A paper machinery company in Georgia keeps a 72-year-old scientist on the payroll just because their customers' scientists like him. Whenever they are scheduling a technical review, they bring out the senior expert and give him a chance to have lunch with his old friends. It always makes the meeting go smoothly.

Skills required of the specialist:

- The specialist must be able to communicate with a wide range of people. Systems analysts may be asked to present to the customer's senior management team, for example.

- The specialist must be able to communicate complex issues to a less informed audience since it will often be necessary for the team to understand and act on the implications of a specialist's recommendations.

The Power Player

Power players are usually senior level executives who can make things happen. They can break the rules or make new ones when it is in the company's best interest. Often with titles like vice president, director, or even CEO, power players can help you internally and externally.

Internally. Internally, power players can make things happen for you within your company. The more ridged your company's internal structure, the more important a sponsor is. If your sale includes multiple departments, having a power player that is above all departments can help you bridge the politics.

A leader in tinted window film also has a division that makes cleaning products. To make a sale of both products to an office building in Miami, the window film sales representative needed the help of two division vice presidents. These internal power players had the ability to get their divisions to work together and allow the rep to sell a combined package.

If your project requires significant internal resources, having the support of internal power players can make the difference between delivering on time and apologizing on your knees.

Externally. Externally, power players can help you gain high-level agreement with customers. While your team may be willing to commit to anything the customer needs, only a senior manager from your company can commit the company to the endeavor. Used properly, your power player can aid in turning a value sale into a relationship sale or a relationship into a partnership. They can also assist in building rapport with their peers on the customer side. This relationship can be invaluable when things get sticky.

When a bank is offering financing to a new company, it is sometimes a visit from the bank president that seals the deal. In her role as power player, the president can offer a level of relationship that no one else, especially the loan officer, can provide.

The key to effective utilization of power players is recognizing that they work for you. If you ask for their help and give them clear directions, they are likely to do what you ask. If you just bring them along, expect them to shoot-from-the-hip and miss the target. Worse, if you forget to include them and they inject themselves into the team, you will risk losing control of the process and the sale.

> Power players work for you.
> Use them wisely.

Skills required of the power player:

- They must be able to work for the team.

- They must exhibit willingness to listen to and take their directions from the team.

- They must have the ability to see their role as that of helping the team move the sale forward through advice and presence.

The Approver

Approvers can say yes or no to a deal. They are, by definition, integral parts of the process on your side. This can be a marketing manager approving the launch of a new service or a director of operations approving a change to the production process. The trick to good team selling is to have the approvers on board as early as possible. The last thing you want is to have the customer say yes and your company say no.

Sometimes approvers don't say yes or no. In fact, the most dangerous ones just string you along and delay your project until the customer cries "Uncle." This is almost always because you did not get them behind the sale from the beginning.

> Get your team behind you or you'll be left out in the cold.

One sales rep took a gamble and sold a new product, without permission, months before the launch date. He hoped his enthusiasm would be rewarded with the first shipments from the new production line. Unfortunately, he did not have the production manager on his side, and he was six months late in delivering to the customer.

Don't forget to sell your approvers on the deal before you sign the contract with the customer.

Skills required of the approver:

- Approvers must be good listeners and concise decision makers. They should be willing to listen to the team's proposal, gather the needed information, and make a decision before too much time and energy is wasted.

- Approvers often need to meet with customers to assess the viability of a project. For this reason, they must also be effective communicators.

Minor Roles

The minor roles fill in the dozens of tasks required to complete your team's work. In smaller companies and smaller sales, many of these roles will be assumed by your team members. In major opportunities, it makes sense for you to add resources that will allow the team to spend time on the customer-related tasks.

Group Representative

In horizontal teams, the group representative is the internal advocate for the division or product group. This role can be filled by a technical specialist, marketing manager, or an account manager. The choice is usually made to accommodate the current phase of the selling cycle.

A company like Monsanto might bring group representatives from their seed, fertilizer, and no-till farming divisions to sell a single account. In fact, as more and more companies attempt to move from vendor relationships to partnerships and long-term relationships, multiple group representation is essential for making the sale. Each group representative is able to speak with authority on his own division while demonstrating that he is part of a well organized, multiproduct service company.

Skills required of the group representative:

- The group representative must have significant knowledge of the group's product or service and how to integrate it with the products or services being sold by the other groups represented in the team.

- A group representative must be willing to play a lead or supporting role, as needed.

Financial Representative

Your financial representative may serve one or more accounting-style roles in the team. In fully self-managed teams, the financial representative is charged with reviewing the profit and loss statement and managing the team's budget. In more typical teams, this role is played by the division controller or her office staff. In this case, the financial representative may not be an active participant in the regular team activities.

Skills required of the financial representative:

- Financial representatives must have an understanding of bookkeeping and/or basic accounting.

- They must have an appreciation for the value of the sale and the costs involved.

Secretary

Like any committee, teams need someone to take notes, post agendas, prepare reports and presentations, and file various types of information. In small- and medium-sized teams, these tasks will be performed by volunteers from within the team. In larger efforts, an administrative assistant may dedicate part of his time to the sales team.

Skills required of the secretary:

- A proficiency with word processing

- A proficiency with presentation software

- A proficiency with electronic communications tools

Figure 3-1
Roles and Responsibilities

Roles	Members						
Major Roles							
Owner							
Scout							
Progress Manager							
Specialist							
Power Player							
Approver							
Minor Roles							
Group Representative							
Financial Representative							
Secretary							
Facilitator							

Complete a separate chart for each different phase of the sale.

Facilitator

One mistake many team leaders make is allowing the owner to run all of the meetings. When you run a meeting, your ideas will have more power than the ideas of others. As a result, some vital team members may prefer to sit back rather than fight a losing battle. Using a

> Fill in the minor roles carefully. They support the entire team.

designated facilitator can level the playing field and ensure that everyone is heard. Facilitators are often chosen as needed from the ranks of those who do not feel passionately about the current issue.

Skills required of the facilitator:

- The ability to draw out and process multiple ideas in a coherent manner

- The ability to help the group reach consensus, clarity, and finality

- The ability to build credibility with the team

Summary

Show your teams the roles and responsibilities outlined in this chapter and then let them arrange the final structure (Figure 3-1). As a leader, you may find it necessary to help the team fill in the gaps or avoid overlapping jobs, but be flexible in your approach. There is no one perfect way to build a sales team, and your team may just discover a twist that works perfectly for their challenge.

4

How to Lead a
Winning Team

It is amazing what can be accomplished when nobody cares about who gets the credit.

Robert Yates

This chapter is for those who will lead sales teams and for those who choose the leaders. Let's not kid ourselves. While it would be nice to think that all teams could be self-managed from the start, the truth is that few teams ever reach that level. Most either succeed under a competent leader or flounder and fail. In many companies, maybe yours, teams are instituted by the corporate edict of a well-meaning and totally clueless CEO. As such, they are thrown together without proper justification, training, or support. I believe this is the reason for the bad name that teaming has acquired. We hopefully can all agree that teaming is not bad; bad teaming is bad!

If your company were to spend its scarce resources on training one group of people, that group should be the sales team leaders. This is because sales team leaders are the cue balls of your sales world. They roll out into the world and make contact with every person involved in the sales effort. Their skills will either motivate or mortify, clarify or confuse the rest of the team. In this chapter, we will examine how leaders should lead and what pitfalls they must avoid. We will also examine the separate problems of managing the remote team, since many sales teams today function under this model.

In our firm's team selling model, team leaders will typically be either the scouts or the progress managers. As the team develops, others may step into the leadership role as necessary. In a major retailer, for example, the leadership role may move from the scout (sales representative) to the progress manager (account manager) and on to the manager of operations or logistics who picks up the role of progress manager.

> Pick your leaders with great care. They often define the success of the team.

Minor leaders are always needed for subteams and special project groups. Whether it is leading the entire team or a small part of it, leadership is fundamentally the same and it is always of critical importance. The role of the leader is to ensure that the right things are done when needed by the right people.

Assessing the Need for Leadership

Some teams, by their very nature, require more leadership than others. Leaders must be able to assess this need as they develop a team to ensure they can devote adequate time to the team. It is often better to forgo a project that is doomed from the start than to waste precious resources and negatively impact moral. Too many lost sales are blamed on the teaming process or the team members, when the true responsibility rested with leadership.

To assess your team's need for leadership, you will need to examine these five factors:

1. Proximity

2. Ability

3. Maturity

4. Diversity

5. Team size

The more factors your team exhibits, the more likely it is to need strong leadership.

Proximity. [1]   Are the members of the team located in the same building or city? If not, the challenges they face in forming an effective unit are multiplied many times. Separated team members often have more difficulty finding time to meet and staying focused. Their meetings are often virtual, requiring video conferencing or teleconferencing. Widely separated team members are less likely to reach the point of true self-management. That said, most of your team members may be dispersed around the country. To be successful, pay particular attention to the communication issues.

Ability.   Ability deals with both the range of skills represented in your team and their competency in those skills. In many cases, teams made up of highly capable individuals will need less leadership than those requiring help at the skill level. In highly functioning teams, the leader's job is to be prepared to move the big rocks out of the road. In other words, only step in when team members lack the power or ability to get the task done.

Maturity.   In Chapter 2, we discussed the stages of team development as organize, define, strategize, and perform.[2] Teams that have experienced this process in the past will, most likely, move through the early stages more quickly and efficiently than beginners. They will also require less intervention on the part of an external team leader. Try to build your team with a few experienced team members to serve as guides to the newer team members.

Diversity.   In this context, diversity applies to the wide array of differences that can cause conflicts and miscommunication in a team. Differences in race, ethnicity, gender, and nationality can be added to differences in knowledge, rank, education, and earnings to create a complex mix. Managers should allow more time to deal with these issues in less experienced teams or situations where diversity has been an issue in the past. While diversity can create problems, it also offers benefits that far outweigh those issues.

> Assess your team's need for leadership, and give your team the gift of a leader who is up to the challenge.

Team size.   While sales teams can range from 2 to 200 members, the core team should be kept as small as possible. As size increases, so do issues with meetings, communication, and consensus. Larger teams require more direct leadership, so smart leaders break large teams into smaller subteams with competent leaders in each one.

Becoming a Great Leader

One of the most common questions asked by both leaders and those who must choose them is, "Who makes a great leader?" It seems that most people paraphrase the old Supreme Court line that says they can't define it, but "they know one when they see one." The problem with this approach is that it is limited by who is doing the selecting. Many of us tend to choose others like us and miss the opportunities beyond our own comfort zone.

At a minimum, your sales team leaders need to have the capability to guide the team from the start to the finish. Leaders need to do this while realizing that it is really the team that is leading and that, for the most part, the leader is simply the aide. Leaders who micromanage or even do the team's work will find themselves busy, alone, and failing.

Team leaders must manage a large number of critical items. Their to-do lists include the following:

Secure resources for the team
Build and maintain trust within the team
Facilitate meetings
Develop the team vision
Negotiate accountabilities
Define performance metrics
Review performance
Facilitate the sharing of ideas
Offer training
Coach and mentor team members

Arbitrate disagreements
Protect the team from outside forces
Serve as liaison to management
Negotiate and manage compensation
Assist in developing a communication plan
Help define the culture
Build a feeling of empowerment
Set boundaries where needed
Identify leaders
Motivate through crisis

It should be clear that many of these jobs will eventually be transferred to the team members, but they will always remain the ultimate responsibility of the leader.

Leading through Influence

Most sales team leaders are managers without power since few, if any, of the team members report to them directly. The leader may have little or no power over members' compensation or input into their next review. While this might not seem like the ideal scenario, it is very often the case and the implications for the manager are significant. Managers who are used to a command style of leadership will find themselves at a severe disadvantage since they will have no leverage.

The good news is that leading through influence is a far better way of managing today's workforce. This shift is encountered far beyond the corporate walls. I was working with a U.S. Army recruitment team and had a colonel in the group for one of the sessions. We were discussing power in leadership, and I asked her how much power her rank gave her. She said, "It gets them on their feet when I enter the room, but after that they start measuring me, just like everyone else, to see what I'm made of." Even in the military, power is a poor substitute for leadership.

Look at it this way: The leader's job is to keep the project on track and to move the big rocks out of the road. Good leaders do for teams what the members cannot do for themselves, and they avoid doing those things that the team members can do for themselves. Leaders have a limited amount of exclusive power. If you are the leader, it is your responsibility to use that power to serve the team.

> **Power is a poor substitute for leadership skills.**

Gaining Respect and Authority

Respect and authority are privileges bestowed on one individual by another. They must be earned and re-earned over time through actions and behaviors that are valued by the team. Whether you are a CEO or the leader of a committee within a team, it is important to exhibit the traits that cause others to support you.

Time magazine's list of the top 20 leaders of the twentieth century included Franklin Delano Roosevelt and Ronald Reagan. Both are known for their ability to get others to follow them through their words and commitment. Both earned and re-earned the nation's respect through their actions. In the end, the most powerful authority a president has is that which is granted to him by a nation that chooses to follow him.

As a leader, you must excel in the following key areas to earn the respect and authority necessary to lead your team.

Be Knowledgeable

People respect those who have the right answers. In fact, while I don't recommend it, those who know a lot can get away with breaking the rules. When I was an engineer at Raytheon, we had a few senior engineers who were brilliant. Everyone deferred to these guys, and they wrote their own rules. The good news is that knowledge is attainable by anyone who is willing to devote the time and energy. You don't need to be politically connected or even chosen for a task to learn more about a specific subject. You can always learn on your own.

Borrow Authority

Authority is often loaned to you by people who rank higher than you do. Learn to use it wisely. For example, let's say that the senior VP of Sales has asked you to get a team together to investigate the potential for business at a particular company. He said, "This is important. Make it a priority!" By all rights, your requests for support on this project carry as much weight as if they came from the VP himself. For this very reason, you should discreetly let it be known whose project this is. After all, if you don't get the support and you are called into the VP's office, won't he ask, "Didn't you tell them that it was important and that it was for me?" Don't be heavy handed with this power and don't use it where you don't need it, but good leaders use the leverage they have to get what they need.

Build Trust

Trust is a powerful asset and one that we also discuss in other chapters. Have you ever worked for someone you did not trust? If so, do you remember how guarded everyone was and how little information changed hands? Like respect, trust must be earned from the people around you. In informal surveys, performed by my company with hundreds of team members around the world, there were four actions that were universally accepted as the keys to building trust with those around you.

1. *Trust others.* In countless surveys on the subject of effective leadership, this is the first criteria people cited. Most of us say we trust those who trust us. As a team leader, this means asking questions rather than giving orders and then letting others try it their way. You must give a little to get a little.

2. *Keep promises.* It can be as simple as promising to bring donuts or as complex as backing someone who is in trouble for something you requested them to do. When you give your word, you should keep it or die trying. On those occasions when you must disappoint your team, give as full an explanation as you can. Let them know why you made the promise and what has changed since that time. They will forgive you if they understand and if you have established a pattern of trust.

3. *Protect confidences.* Leaders often hear information that is private or confidential. Trustworthy people keep this knowledge to themselves until they have permission to share it. Once you get a reputation for loose lips, your access to information will be shut down. This is something a leader can't afford.

4. *Do more than expected.*   Our surveys also tell us that trust extends to your accomplishment too. People trust those who do what is required, and a little more. This makes sense since it allows others to have confidence in the quality of the work you will do.

Build Individuals

There is a basic rule of life that says: If you want to be a getter, be a giver. This is as true in leading teams as anywhere else. If you want to gain the respect of others, help them accomplish their goals. One way to do this is to help team members grow through their position on the team. Ask members what they would like to learn as a result of this experience and do your best to position them to gain the knowledge or experience they seek.

Managers with a reputation for building individuals never seem to have trouble finding great performers for their teams. Not only do good people want to join them, but they have built a network of people who have improved their skills and are ready for the next opportunity.

When one CEO was recently profiled in a business journal, the writer interviewed people who had worked with him over the years. The consistent message was this: I am better today because I worked with him. Each felt they had grown under this CEO's leadership.

You can help your people grow by

- Training, which will bring new skills to those in need of them. Every team can use training in some area. Make sure you assess the members' needs and budget the time and money for effective training programs.

- Coaching, which will help individuals or small groups apply new skills in the workplace until they become habits. Coaching takes time, so it is often focused on the most interested parties. You can teach small groups to coach one another too.

- Mentoring, which will help individuals plan their development path and guide them as they follow it. Mentoring is highly time intensive for the leader and therefore must be reserved for those individuals who show great promise. Mentoring programs can be established within the company to provide opportunities for anyone who is willing to commit the time and energy.

Leverage Your Contacts

In my team selling classes, I pose this scenario: "You are a manager, and you want Bill to work on your team. Bill says he is too busy and can't help, but you still want his help. What do you do?"

The typical response is, "Ask his boss to order him to do it!" Unfortunately, this common answer is wrong. Let's assume you do go over Bill's head and his boss says yes. Congratulations, you now have an angry Bill on your team.

A better approach would be to leverage your contacts. Ask Bill what other commitments he has made and who controls the priorities on those tasks. Next, get Bill's permission to approach those contacts and propose reprioritizing Bill's workload to make time for your work. Bill might even go with you to explain how it could all be done. If successful, you now have a happy Bill on board. Work through people, not over them.

Organize the Process

Team selling definitely has a process and organizational side to it. Because of the number of people involved, it goes far beyond the one-on-one sales process that many of us learned. As a result, it is incumbent on the leader to help the team understand the new techniques and to ensure that an organized process is observed by all.

Here are three steps that any leader can use with their team to help them learn to apply the team selling process effectively:

1. *Clarify the process.* The leader must aid the team in defining their process and ensure that it is clear for all to follow.

2. *Gain agreement on roles, responsibilities, and rules.* The leader helps the team gain agreement on the roles, responsibilities, and rules they will work by. The leader must be willing to set limits where needed to ensure both a successful outcome and compliance with company guidelines.

3. *Ensure responsibilities are assigned precisely.* While the team may believe they have defined a process and divided the tasks clearly, the leader must be able to identify ambiguities, contradictions, and gaps in their assignments.

A sales manager for a regional telephone company decided to use team selling as a way to increase sales at major accounts. She had individual reps calling on the account for long-distance services, equipment sales, Internet services, video conferencing, and local lines. First, she brought them together to show them how team selling might work and what the process might look like. She gained their support and worked with the team to define their roles and responsibilities. As the team moved into action, she checked in to see that the responsibilities had been assigned correctly and that the team was functioning effectively and efficiently. By working with the team as they developed, the leader was able to guide them through the understanding and implementation of a new way of selling.

Negotiate Effectively

To be a leader, you must be a competent negotiator. Leaders negotiate with their team members, with other teams, with management, and with the client. They negotiate roles, rules, compensation, resources, timetables, specifications, vacations, and much more. The key factor that makes leaders' negotiations unique is that, regardless of the outcome of the negotiations, they must work again tomorrow with the people they negotiate with today. For that reason, win-win is the only option.

Throughout your team's life, you will have times when the team's schedule is less demanding. Take advantage of these opportunities to earn favors with other departments. Offer to give them a hand when you can and set your team up for the help it will need in the future. You might also tell departments who are supporting you that they can put your tasks on a lower priority for a while. The shock value alone is worth the effort.

It is very common for the best people to be busiest just when you need them on your team. Rather than insisting that the prime people be fully dedicated to your team, why not compromise? Determine where in your process the top person is needed and try to minimize your use of that person. Everyone, especially the top person, will appreciate your effort, you'll probably get more than you asked for, and your fellow team members will be happy to give it.

One of the best negotiating techniques is simply listening. Listen to determine what is important to other people and try to frame your need in such a way that they get what they want. Let's suppose you need time from the machine shop but the manager is being difficult to work with. Further imagine that the machine shop is working hard to justify their budget and afraid of cuts. If you get the use of the machines and your sale is successful, it could mean millions to the company. Why not offer to write a letter to the CEO crediting the machine shop for your sale? You get the commission, and they get the credit. This is just another example of a win-win outcome created by an experienced leader.

Motivate with Courtesy

A leader must be able to take a team to the next level in performance through effective motivational techniques. Nothing is easier to lead than a team that wants to follow you. A good motivator gets people to happily do something that they would not otherwise want to do. While there are many great techniques for motivation, the simplest is often the best. Identify what the members of the team want, and show them how to get it. This can be as simple as recognition for a job well done or lunch out with the boss. Ask enough questions and the answers will become obvious.

Encourage Risk Taking

Many of us are risk-averse by training. Our teachers, parents, and previous bosses may have beaten the risk-taking genes right out of us. While you, as a leader, must maintain a balanced ship, you must also encourage your team to try new approaches. Leaders must constantly encourage their teams to expand their thinking with what-if questions.

> Respect and authority are best earned intentionally by consistent actions.

The key to encouraging risk is to accept failure with grace. The key to killing future risk taking is being instantly critical when something goes wrong. It's your choice. Choose risk!

Changing Focus of the Leader[3]

As your team develops, your role as the leader will change accordingly. If you are to nurture your team's growth, you must continually shift your focus. In the early stages of development, the leader's focus will be internal to the team. This focus is required because the team needs immediate guidance and attention if it is to form properly. As the team matures, the leader shifts his focus to the external view. Here, he can help the team acquire resources and defend against outside interference.

Finally, the leader hovers like a helicopter over a work site. The leader stays far enough away to let the team function and grow, yet close enough to be called in when needed. It is in this hovering stage that the team and the team leader may experience the most difficult and yet most important growth. Hover too close and the team will be dependent on you and never move toward self-management. Hover too far and the team may get so far off course that the goals are in jeopardy.

George Mozek, one of my favorite sales managers and mentors, said that leading was like a parent watching a child play with eggs on a table. The parent sees one egg roll toward the edge of the table. If the parent reaches out to stop it, the child will never learn to exercise that particular skill for himself or herself. If not, the egg will certainly break.

The skillful leader stands back and lets the team members learn from their mistakes. The leader also knows which eggs to let the team learn on and which ones must be protected at all costs. The best way for a manager to know where to be is to ask. Your team will tell you if they need more room or more support. Trust them, and then check up on the important details.

> Check in with your team by asking, "How am I doing?" Then be prepared to listen and change.

Summary

Leadership is a skill that must be constantly honed if the leader is to be effective. In team selling, leaders can make the difference between success and failure. By periodically examining your style, effectiveness, and goals, you can use the team process as a training ground to improve your talents. Just as sales representatives regularly learn new techniques for prospecting and presenting, their team leaders must constantly learn new techniques to help their team become the best it can be.

5

How to Contribute to a Winning Team

If everyone is thinking alike, then somebody isn't thinking.
General George S. Patton

If you are a member of a sales team, you may have skipped Chapter 4 on leading a team. That's OK because this chapter is for you. While much is made of the leadership roles in teams, far more is done by the members of the teams than by the leaders. This chapter is devoted to exploring ways for the team members to become as effective as possible and have fun doing it. After all, teaming should be the most enjoyable way to work.

Define Your Own Role

As a team member, you play the role most critical to the success of your team for two reasons. First, because you do the lion's share of the work; and second, because you are closest to the situations that matter and have the opportunity to collect the best information. With knowledge comes responsibility and so the team members are not simply along for the ride but are the critical components of the sales team. As a sales team member, you must always think of yourself as an advocate for both the client and the company.[1]

Because individual sales team members are the key to a sale's success, you have a wide range of roles. I have attempted to summarize these roles below, but I am certain that this list is far from exhaustive. Each team must take the time to determine what roles will be required for the team to be successful. Make a list for your team and ensure that each role is defined, assigned, and supported by the rest of the group. Here are descriptions of eight key roles to get you started.

Initiator

When I was in college, Dr. Strait, dean of the School of Engineering at Syracuse University, offered me a piece of sage advice. He said that there are two types of workers: those who dutifully do the work that is given to them and those who seek out the meaningful work they want to do. This single piece of advice made more of a difference in my career than any other. As a team member, you should not wait to be assigned something to do; you must be part of the process of defining your own work. You must seek out the important work that needs to be done.

You must pick up the responsibilities that others drop and fill in the gaps as you find them. In the process you will choose for yourself the interesting tasks that make the job more fun.

If the leader runs the team correctly, he or she will ask for input from your team and use each team member as a resource. If the leader fails to do this, you and the other team members must initiate the process.

I have often found that team members tend to be pretty tough on their leaders. They expect them to be better at leading than many of them are. Let's cut your leader a break! Leaders are often thrust into positions of responsibility with little training or preparation. That's

> Each team member is responsible for taking action when he or she sees the need.

why it is critical for the team members to help them do their jobs by initiating discussions and action when required. When a team member sees something the leader should know or should be doing, he should speak up. The best leaders are the best listeners, but someone else has to be saying something important.

Reporter

Team members are the eyes and ears of the company. As they are working with clients and other departments, they collect information that is critical to the success of the sale or the customer relationship. When not shared with the team, this information is worthless. Team members should never assume that someone else already knows what they know or that it's not their job to inform others. In fact, most knowledge is lost, not because it is not gathered but because it is never passed along, and many sales are lost for lack of knowledge.

In team selling, the specialists are often the ones who are given the golden information. A buyer might never tell a sales representative about a competitor's products, but in the lab, one engineer will gladly show another the full details of the other company's offering. I am not suggesting that anyone ever do anything unethical, but information freely given is yours to use and share. The more effective your team's observing and reporting system is, the more information you will be able to use in making the sale.

In many sales situations, the sales team will be actively seeking specific types of information. Here, the team members should develop a list of the data required by the group so they are listening for that information during client meetings and site visits. One simple example is that of a trade show.

Each member of the team has identified particular buyers or other decision makers who have been difficult to contact. Since these contacts are likely to be on the exhibit floor of the show, each member of the team should be supplied with a list of their names and the corresponding team member. When one of the contacts is located, team members can either introduce themselves or find the appropriate team member and let them make contact. Working as a well-organized group, your sales team can gather far more information from many more contacts than would be possible otherwise.

> Knowledge is only powerful when it is shared with others.

Contrarian

In a discussion, the least valuable person in the room is often the one who agrees with you. In fact, if everyone is in agreement you might wonder if you need the discussion. Contrarians improve the outcomes of discussions by challenging the assumptions and forcing others to defend their decisions. Teams function best when there is a spirit of open discussion and healthy debate. Challenges must not be seen as negative attacks but as positive ways to improve the decision-making process.

As team members, you must develop the skills to challenge an idea without attacking the person who initiated it. In sensitive situations where a public challenge is inappropriate, it is appropriate to ask for permission to "think it over" and then arrange a time for a one-on-one discussion. Trust your feelings in these situations and

> Improvement requires someone to challenge the conventional thinking.

be sensitive to individuals who might not be as thick-skinned as you. If you sense that you might have bruised someone's ego or stepped on his toes, be sure to apologize. Apologies cost very little, and they buy a ton of goodwill on the team.

Since constructive feedback is critical to your success, team members will want to encourage it from teammates. Appendix B contains suggestions for ways to maximize the quantity and quality of feedback. These techniques work because they recognize the differences in the way people think and act and allow for each to respond in his or her own way.

Clarifier

Have you ever heard two people arguing and discovered that they were actually on the same side of the argument? One says "heads" and the other says "not tails," and they both miss the point that they are already in agreement. Team members who are able to clarify a situation are a valuable asset to the team.

Clarifiers come in other styles too. They can help explain complex systems and issues in terms that others can understand. Given that your sales team will be composed of very talented technical, sales, and marketing people, it is quite likely that each will speak in his or her own industry language. Furthermore, each will bring to your team a set of complex ideas and proposals that will need to be understood by every member. Team members who have the ability to understand all sides and bring clarity to the discussion will be valuable assets to the group.

When I learned to rock climb, the instructor told each of us that we were individually responsible for clear communication and that clear communication would save our lives. He was right. As we learned the basic commands, each command was paired with a response that let the other climbers know that the commands had been heard and understood. These pairs of commands and responses could be heard all over the climbing area and everyone knew what they meant. Our instructor had broken down a complex and dangerous activity into a clear process that could easily be understood by a beginner. Through the programmed responses, he also gave us a way to clarify our own process without his being present.

> The true skill of communication is the ability to explain the complex to the uninformed.

As a team member, you should listen for the need to clarify definitions, instructions, communication, or misunderstanding. If each member pitches in, the entire team will benefit.

Recorder

If you have ever been on a committee at a religious institution or an association, you know that someone has to take the minutes.

Even in a small group of people who meet face-to-face on a regular basis, some sort of written record is needed for reference when questions arise. In sales teams there are official and unofficial recorders. The responsibilities of the official recorder are covered in the meetings section of Chapter 10. Here we are interested in the unofficial recorders.

Everyone who communicates becomes an unofficial recorder for the team. E-mails, memos, plans, proposals, and even records of phone conversations are sales team records. So are updates to sales force automation (SFA) and customer relationship management (CRM) systems. As a team member, your job is to make sure you comply with the team's communication protocols and share your information freely. You should also keep good records of information you gather, meetings you attend, and ideas that develop. It's often said that a poor pencil and paper is better than a great memory. When in doubt, record it!

When I started working on the Patriot missile as a young engineer at Raytheon many years ago, I was issued a blank notebook. I was told to record all my notes and do all my work in that book. Every time I filled one, they gave me a new one. Over the years, I have maintained this habit and it has paid off many times. As a result, I know what I said, what I promised, what I need to do, and what others owe me. I know what my clients needed last year, so I can match them to our new products this year.

> The person who writes it down for others to share makes it happen.

It is important to note that records are for positive, not negative, purposes. We have all heard countless people use their records as a way of reducing their responsibility in the event of a future problem. The standard comment is, "If anything happens, I wrote it down so I'm covered." What this really means is that this person has a documented excuse to protect him from blame.

Since none of us have "collect excuses" in our job descriptions, let's take another approach. Whenever you see something that might go wrong in the future, be an initiator and speak up. Do the best you can to fix the situation as early as possible, rather than simply recording it for future use.

Historian

Most of your sales opportunities originate from some previous activity. Having a history of past relationships with clients, products, divisions, or partners is important to understanding the context in which things occur. As a member of the team it is your job to volunteer the history that you know and seek out historical information that might be helpful to the team. The more teams you are on, the more history you will bring to each group. Other sources of historical information include former employees, employees who have worked for the client company, and those who worked with the account but have been promoted or moved out of the selling arena.

A good example is a team that was negotiating with a major client who wanted the selling company to spend tooling dollars up front, with their profit being made on the units we would process for the client. The sales representative was arguing to his company that they should do it since it would lock up the business. The operations manager was afraid that the client would not come through on their end of the deal. After consulting with another senior manager who had negotiated with this client for years, they discovered that this was a game the

> Listen to those who have been there before you.

customer played often and one that was seldom a good deal for the vendor. As a result of that valuable historical advice, the sales team renegotiated the deal and won the contract.

Unfortunately, some teams intentionally leave experienced people off the team. This may be due to a leader's desire to work from a clean slate or the reputation that the historian has as a negative or overpowering personality. In either case, the sales will progress more effectively if the team members find a way to bring all relevant history to the sales process. While it might be nice to have a clean slate, it is seldom the reality.

Cheerleader

Several years ago, my wife worked for L.L. Bean's corporate sales department. One day, as they moved into their busy season, her boss asked her to be the department cheerleader. What a great idea to actually appoint someone to bring some fun and balance into the organization. I have a simple rule: If it's not fun, don't do it. In reality many things are not naturally fun, but they can

> A great team is a positive team. Be the one who makes it happen.

be made more enjoyable if we think about it. Studies have shown that people do better work when they are having a good time. We also know that clients buy from people they like, and I assume they like people who are having fun doing their jobs.

Cheerleaders should recognize all types of successes. Take time to congratulate the person who made the sale, the great presentation, or the wonderful report. Nothing is more motivating than the recognition of your peers. If each of us takes a turn at the cheerleader role, the job will feel less like work and the client will feel less like a client and more like a friend.

Water Carrier

OK, there are junk jobs to do. That's what one of the special-needs kids I worked with called them. He was proud of his work, but he knew he was doing the tasks that others wanted to avoid: "junk jobs." In every sales team there will be undesirable tasks that someone must do. Whether it is flying to Anchorage for a meeting in January (I did that) or completing sales and expense reports, the work must get done. As a member of the team, you must volunteer for your share of these unpleasant tasks. In fact, the best team members volunteer for more than their share and are often rewarded with the better trips and other benefits. Be a water carrier, do the junk jobs, and you'll sleep better at night.

> If you want to be a getter, be a giver!

Get on Board

As a new team member, you may be joining a newly formed team or one already in progress. In either case, you can only do your best for the team if you understand the objectives of the job and the deliverables that are expected of you.

The objective is best explained as "why we are doing this." A typical sales team might be attempting to increase sales at an existing account by 20 percent over the next year or penetrating a new account to generate $2.5 million in sales over the next 18 months. Each task assigned within the team should be tied to the overall goal. Each task should also have a set of defined deliverables. A typical deliverable might be to develop an organizational chart of the company with responsibilities and contact information. Your first job is to clarify your deliverables to ensure that you are accurately supporting the needs of the team. Ask who, what, where, when, how, and why. You'll need to know who should be included in your meetings, what database should be used to record information, where the team's notes are kept, and so on. It's your job to ask for what you need to know to do the job right. It's your job to find the details.

> It's your job to bring yourself up to speed.

This is important because many leaders forget to bring new members up to speed or they assume that everyone knows the objectives. You can do any task better and with more energy if you understand and believe in the goal. Make it your job to "get yourself on board" and become the best team member you can.

Here are the five most effective things you can do to get yourself on board quickly:

1. Meet informally with the leader and other team members to ask questions and begin an open relationship.

2. Review the team's correspondence file, especially team meeting minutes.

3. Meet with the client to introduce yourself. Admit that you are new and are looking for ways to be of service.

4. Make sure you are on all relevant distribution lists for e-mail and important documents.

5. Review the client research file, their Web site, annual report, recent press releases, and stock price activity.

Armed with this information, you will be prepared to participate as a key member of the team.

Assess Your Teammates

As a team member you will have to rely on other members of the team for a wide range of tasks. If you want to be successful, you will need to be able to assess the capabilities of your team members. You will need to know what they know and what experience they bring to the team. Essentially, you need a short biography of each member. Far too often I have been surprised to find the resource I needed right under my nose.

You should recommend that each team member complete a resume for the team. It should include previous jobs, important projects, major accounts, and personal strengths. You especially want to know about their experience with the client you are working on, such as information about the client's competitors and industry. You also want to learn about hobbies, travel, academic experience, and awards. Civic involvement can even be important to include. Post these resumes with photos on your intranet for the team to access.

> Get to know your team members quickly.

The results will amaze you. The wealth of experience and knowledge that is sitting around your meeting table is impressive and so are the number of unique experiences that may play a part in future discussions. Whether it is finding a rock climber to spend a day with an adventurous CEO or identifying someone who was elected to the town council and knows how to sell to a public group, this will be worth the effort. As a side benefit, it will build the team through the exposure of shared experiences.

Lead from Within the Team

As a team develops, all members become leaders. In fully self-managing teams, the leadership role moves around the team at a dizzying speed as each member leads his or her particular area of interest.

If you are a new team member and have never lead anything before, you should understand that all leaders start with one thing: the willingness to work with people to make something happen. Start small.

Here are eight key tasks that you can take on as beginning leadership positions:

1. Volunteer to lead a sales team meeting.

2. Organize a client meeting.

3. Organize the report to senior management.

4. Lead a group in client research.

5. Lead the group that is preparing a proposal.

6. Lead the planning for an upcoming presentation.

7. Brief the new team members.

8. Handle a problem with another division.

Each of the many activities within the team requires leadership and offers a place for new team members to improve their skills and show others their capabilities. In my team selling seminars, I seldom hear anyone complain about leading,

> Everyone can be, and should be, a leader.

but I often hear complaints about poor leadership. My advice is always the same. If you don't like your leaders, take your turn at leading. You will probably fix a few problems and, at the same time, gain a newfound respect for the position.

What Is Consensus?

While a dictionary definition of *consensus* might read, "an opinion or position reached by a group as a whole," the practical team definition is slightly more useful. Teams typically define consensus as a decision, reached by a group, which can be supported by the group as a whole. This means that everyone does not have to agree with the decision, but everyone must be able to support it. A team member's job is to pick his or her battles and support the team when possible. To quote the Rolling Stones, "You can't always get what you want. But if you try sometime, you just might find you get what you need."

> Consensus making is everyone's job.

When you disagree with a position and are questioning whether you should fight it, ask yourself these five questions:

1. Is this important to reaching the team's goals?

2. Could the other idea work if amended?

3. Is there a clear compromise position you could propose?

4. Is this a violation of your principles or ethics?

5. Is there additional information that you can offer to help the team decide?

In some way, you are in it for yourself. That's not necessarily a bad thing if self-interest does not dominate the decision making of the group. If you get something you want, then you will feel satisfied and motivated to support others. Give in when you can and stand your ground when you should. Consensus can only be reached when everyone is flexible. Be a consensus maker when you can, but never give up the goals or your principles.

Overcome Personality Conflicts

Sales teams are the ultimate in cross-functional teams. As such, they are composed of individuals with widely varying backgrounds, education, processing styles, and goals. If you have been working with sales teams for any time and have not experienced a "personality conflict," you probably have not been looking.

Personality conflicts are characterized by two people who feel they are not able to work together because they are too different. This is a special case of conflict because the parties often do not believe there is anything to work out. They honestly think the other person is just too different for there ever to be a workable solution. In other words, they can't even agree to work on the problem.

In my experience with hundreds of sales teams, there is almost never a true personality conflict. Inevitably, the source of the problem can be reduced to behaviors exhibited by one or both of the parties.

Here is an example:

ENGINEER: "That account rep is a jerk! I can't work with him. He lies to the customers and makes promises we can never keep. He just wants his commission and the heck with the rest of us!"

ACCOUNT REP: "That engineer is a jerk! I can't work with him. He never communicates with the client, and I can never get a commitment date out of him. All he wants to do is play in the lab and to heck with the rest of us!"

You may be laughing now because you have experienced this very conflict. OK, let's deal with it. In this scenario the two parties will seldom be able to resolve the issue by themselves. Another member of the team, the leader, or a human resources representative is needed to facilitate the discussion I am about to propose.

Ask both parties to write down the behaviors that the other person exhibits that bothers them. They must be kept to behaviors and avoid name-calling.

The engineer might write of the account rep:

    Poor attention to details
    Too quick to make decisions
    Makes unrealistic commitments to clients
    Greedy (strike that one, it's not a behavior)

The account rep might write of the engineer:

    Never commits to completion dates
    Too slow to respond to inquiries
    Incompetent (strike that one, it's not a behavior)
    Tells client information he doesn't need to know

The arbitrator now asks both parties if they could work with the other if the issues they wrote down were improved. In most cases the answers are yes from both parties. At this point, you know it is not a "personality" issue but a behavior issue since it is behaviors that they have written down. Gain the agreement of both parties to work together pending improvement of the issues in conflict. Also gain their agreement to work on a resolution of the issues in conflict. Once you focus on specific behaviors and not on personalities, you will find that you are discussing items that can be changed. With both parties agreeing to work toward a

> Most "personality conflicts" can be resolved with a simple process.

solution and the specific changes clearly defined, each party is left with the ability to make adjustments that can resolve the conflict. I do not want to minimize the difficulty in dealing with these issues, but if you follow this process, you will have remarkable results.

Working for Multiple Bosses

The problem of reporting to multiple bosses surfaces often in the companies I consult with. Team members, who work for more than one boss, often on different teams, run into conflicting requests for their time and attention. Each boss wants his or her task to be number one, and there are only so many hours in a day. Even the most committed workers will run out of time eventually.

In most cases, the issue is resolved by the worker, who makes a decision to delay one job in favor of the other. The decision is often based on which boss is liked most or which boss is less likely to scream when the project is late. If these tasks are important to company sales, the worker may now be determining which project will be successful and which will fail. How many companies want their quarterly results left up for grabs like that?

The Sensible Priorities Process

Here is an approach we call the *sensible priorities process* because it is fairer to both the team member and the boss. It also ensures that the actions taken will more accurately reflect the needs and goals of the company.

> When you are squeezed between dueling priorities, speak up and resolve the conflict.

Instruct team members who work on multiple teams for different managers to work with their managers when conflicts over priorities arise. Faced with the reality that something must give, the team member has two options:

1. The team member can ask one manager to exchange the priority of the new task with that of any other task assigned by the same manager. In this way, the inter-manager conflict is avoided and the manager is setting the priorities based on his or her knowledge of the division's goals.

2. If the only way to satisfy the newest request is to move it ahead of a task promised to another manager, ask the two managers to discuss the priorities and decide on the order of work. Once again, the order of work will be determined by those at a level to understand the consequences any shift in priorities will have on the goals of the division or department.

For the sensible priorities process to work there must be agreement and support from team leaders and managers. Without this support, the team members will again be placed in the middle and pressured to make decisions that are beyond their capabilities.

Summary

Being a member of a sales team requires you to be an active, and even a proactive, person. You will be responsible not only for the tasks that are assigned to you but for the unassigned tasks you discover along the way. When you participate in a sales team, you are expected to play an individual role and a team role in an effort to ensure that the goals of the team, your company, and your customer are realized.

6

Value Selling with Teams

Price is what you pay. Value is what you get.

Warren Buffett

Today's top sales professionals know that simply selling features and benefits, being customer focused, or even having a win-win attitude is not sufficient for success. Today you must use "value selling" to show your customer that you have real, provable value. Team selling is the ideal format for conveying value in complex, major account or enterprise-wide sales.

Typically, value selling has been the domain of the sales representative who is responsible for determining need and identifying corresponding value propositions. As effective as this has been, team selling multiplies the power of value selling many times. Each team member now has the opportunity to identify value matches and present value propositions throughout the customer's organization. Done correctly, a value-based team selling approach is nearly unstoppable.

While value selling has traditionally been taught exclusively to sales professionals, you will soon see how every member of your team can play an important part in a sale when they understand value selling.

What Is Value Selling?

Value selling is a process that shows your customers why it is in their best interest to buy from you and to do it now. In value selling, you analyze your offering by how it will affect your customer's business, not by what it was designed to do. Few customers can resist a proposition that proves that a dollar spent today will return two dollars tomorrow. This type of sound business proposal will often cause a CEO or other senior manager with P&L responsibility to loosen the purse strings and authorize the purchase of your product or service.

> Value selling is effective because it shows the customers how they will profit from your solution.

In this chapter, you will see how to use value selling with your team to expand your perceived value to the customer. You will learn how teams can expand your value proposition to the point where your offer is irresistible. Please remember that when I make a claim like that, I am assuming that you have picked your prospects well and that they actually need what you are selling. The difference between the selling game and a con game is ethics. Let's all agree to keep them high.

Defining Value

The first step in value selling is to identify your value in the eyes of the prospect. Your value will differ from customer to customer and from person to person within the customer company. You will find that each member of the team may have a different perceived value to the various contacts each has with the customer. The goal is to identify as much value as possible and add it all up for the customer.

To help with this process, we have developed the value scope to help you find your multiple values as seen by each of your customers. The *value scope* is a 360-degree look at your customer that can serve as a tool for you to use in your team's strategic analysis. It is a top-down look at your customer, represented by a circle or compass. As you look at the customer from each angle, you will be prompted to see the value you offer in many different ways.

As a rule, senior managers of every department are interested in the financial welfare of their company, division, or project. They spend countless hours in meetings reviewing microscopic numbers on giant wall-size spreadsheets. Their fate rests in the size (and direction) of one or two of the numbers on the bottom line. If you know which numbers are important to those decision makers and can show them how to improve them, you become their hero! This is one of the keys to the power of team selling. Your team can develop a unique value proposition for each of the decision makers in the customer's buying group. When you cover enough of these bases effectively, you win!

Value buyers are looking for one of several financial benefits from every purchase. The simplest way to look at value is that your product or service must improve one of the big three:

1. Efficiency

2. Effectiveness

3. Speed

Build Value through Efficiency

Your product or service may improve efficiency if it reduces the cost of the operation or increases the output of the operation. Is your product cheaper to own? Can you help them perform their process with lower costs or less waste? Can you help them get more production out of the same equipment or personnel? To sell efficiency, you should understand the customer's current costs and throughput and be prepared to present proven numbers that support the improvements they can expect from using your product or service.

I was selling a reliability screening program to IBM many years ago. It was a process that they had not used and one for which they did not see the need. Our team met with their team to collect information and help them identify areas where our experience could be helpful to their manufacturing process. Our production engineer discovered that they were having a reject problem with one type of part. So many parts were testing as bad in their receiving inspection that the production line was running short of parts and had to be stopped.

> If you can help them do it cheaper, you can justify the sale.

We were then able to show them how we could prescreen these parts and ensure a steady flow of products to their line. The value they saw was the elimination of the production downtime that the bad parts were causing. Compared with those costs, our fees were minimal and we earned the contract on our efficiency value.

You may need someone in the production department to help you gather these numbers or you may simply need to learn enough about their current process to estimate them. This is where your team comes in. When your production expert meets with their production expert, they will discuss details that would seldom be available to a salesperson. More peer-to-peer contacts mean more information and more opportunities to understand the customer's needs. As you learn how to improve the customer's efficiency, you will be directly helping their bottom line. When you can prove it, your team will win the sale!

Build Value through Effectiveness

Effectiveness is a quality measure, and it relates to the value of the output in the eyes of your customer's customer. Can you show them how to make their product or service better or more valuable to their customer? Will this improvement result in greater sales or higher prices? To improve effectiveness you must understand your customer's product or service and how it competes in the marketplace.

Several years ago, newspaper printers were faced with a problem. Their customers wanted to brag about recycling, but the ink on the paper was toxic. The ink companies worked on the problem and produced a soy-based ink that not only eliminated the recycling problem but also reduced the ink that transferred onto the readers' hands. Press owners saw these benefits, or "effectiveness values," as ways to sell more printing to more newspapers and jumped on the new ink.

> If you can help them do it better, you can justify the sale.

You should be prepared to showcase studies that support your assumptions so that users will see value in the improvements.

Your team's marketing and technical experts will be valuable in collecting the information and research needed here. Effectiveness is value and shows up in the customer's bottom line. Prove it and your team will win the sale.

Build Value through Speed

As technology forces change at an increasingly rapid pace, speed becomes a more and more important value measure. Market opportunities open and close in a virtual instant, and those who can respond can capture a larger share of the fleeting dollars. Being late to market means more than merely missing an opportunity. Being late can mean millions of dollars tied up in worthless inventory and dollars that are not available to spend on other, more profitable opportunities. Can you show your customer how your product or service will speed them to market? Can you deliver an instant, flawless product or service that will get them ahead of the competition while the market is still hot?

A leading mortgage company was outsourcing some if its software programming during the Y2K conversion. A human resources specialist for the vendor who was securing the programmers overheard one of the customer's managers commenting that there was a huge opportunity the company could capture if they could only increase their programming capability by three or four times. The HR manager brought the issue back to her company's sales group, and they developed a plan. They offered to outsource the programming to their division in India and quadruple the mortgage company's current capacity. The deal was successful, and as a result, the mortgage company was able to buy several of their competitors who did not have a Y2K solution and lock up market share for many years to come. Value through speed made the outsourcing worth almost any price.

You will need to present a high level of commitment from your company if you want your customer to believe

> If you can help the customer do it faster, you can justify the sale.

that you will be able to support them in the speed game. This is the time to bring out your team's power players for a high-level presentation. Only C-level and senior managers can make the type of commitments that will make the customer feel comfortable here. Speed is value and shows up on the bottom line. Succeed at this and your team will win the sale!

In each of these cases, you must be prepared to present the numbers as if you worked for the customer company. That means you must understand how their operation works and the costs involved. While this may sound like a daunting task, it is the only way to guarantee success. Over and over we see salespeople dazed and confused because customers, who had frozen all spending, make major purchases from their competitors. What happened? Someone got to a senior manager and showed them how spending now would result in a better-looking bottom line in the very near future. Using the power of the team, you can gather the information, prepare your case, and win the sale!

Using the Value Scope

The goal in selling value is to show the value from as many perspectives as possible. Ideally, you would like everyone involved in the buying decision to see a solid, bottom-line justification for buying from you. To illustrate the process of developing the complete value profile, we will use the value scope (Figure 6-1).

Figure 6-1
Value Scope Model

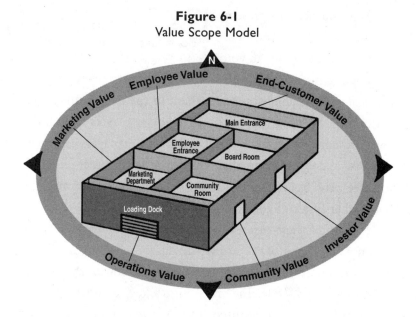

End-Customer Value

We will start by looking in from the northeast. We are looking at the front door, where your customer's customers come in. By helping our customer serve their customer, we are valuable to the customer. To determine your value here, have someone on your team interview some of your customer's customers and ask what they really want from that product or service. Read trade journals and their competitors' Web sites for more clues. The newspaper ink example used earlier is a perfect example of value in this area.

Investor Value

Let's move around the circle to the southeast. This is the side door, the one that leads to the board room and is used by the investors. What do they want, and how can we help our customer deliver? Have your CEO or VP meet with their CEO or

VP and get to know their business needs. Read their annual report and SEC filings on the Security and Exchange Commission's Edgar Web site (*www.sec.gov*). During a lunch meeting with the senior VP of a customer, I learned that they were solely focused on building market share in an effort to boost the resale price of the company. To them, short-term profits were far less important than new customers. They were happy to buy sales training that cost more than the short-term sales would justify because they understood the value each new customer meant to the ultimate sale. Having friends in high places is critical for your team.

Community Value

Moving down the same side of the building, you find the community meeting room. What community does your customer live in or sell in, and how does it affect them? Communities can be the actual city they live in or nongeographic communities, such as unions, public interest groups, or trade organizations. Research news clippings and press releases to uncover hidden community pressures that may be affecting the customer. Oil tankers have moved to double hulls, dairies buy growth-hormone-free milk, and McDonald's has reduced the fat content of their French fries, all because they believe that improved public perception will help them with their bottom lines. Assign someone on your team to investigate the various communities your customer affects and learn what matters to them.

Operations Value

Moving around to the southwest, you come to the back of the building. This is the loading dock, where you and other suppliers deliver your products and services. The obvious values here are features like price, quality, service, and reliability. But there is more. Can you prepackage multiple products to save time and cost? Can you ship in their containers or prelabel products to save them one step in the factory? These value points might be obvious to someone with operations experience, but how many others might miss them. With a production or operations expert on your team you could learn how some of these relatively small issues can have enormous value to the customer. The objective of this story is to show you the importance of getting your experts a tour of the plant!

Marketing Value

Around the circle to the northwest we find the marketing offices. The marketing department is concerned with their company's position in the marketplace. Your insight into the market could help them add new features to their products or services. One of my teams showed a customer how to make their device tamper resistant and gain FDA approval in the hospital market. It earned them millions of dollars and put them years ahead of the competition. This simple suggestion came from an engineer on a sales team who had worked in a hospital and was aware of the problem. Once again, a team can make a sale that an individual might lose.

Employee Value

Our last stop is the employee entrance on the same side of the building. We know that people buy to achieve both company and personal goals. What are the goals of the people you are selling to? How are their bonuses paid? Will they be proud to do business with you? If your team talks with enough people, you may uncover hidden conflicts with the current suppliers that are causing employee unrest. I once had a customer tell me that he would never change vendors for a particular product for one big reason. As he put it, "I never lose sleep over those guys."

The Power Is in the Answers

As they analyze each area, all team members must ask themselves if their offering has value to this contact or department. Here is a list of questions that the team must answer in order to maximize their value to the client.

- Who on our team is best positioned to determine our value in this area?

- What information do we need to gather to determine our value?

- What value do we offer?
  - How can we quantify it?
  - How can we prove it?
  - Who on the customer side is most likely to appreciate the value we offer?
  - How can we arrange to present our value to the right audience?
  - Who on our team should be the one to make the contact/presentation?

- What obstacles must we overcome?
  - Why would the customer resist our value offer?
  - Who on the customer side would see this value as a negative?
  - How can we position ourselves to neutralize them?

> There are many ways your product or service can be of value to a customer.

As you build your team, look at the customer and match the potential value areas with experts on your team. As your team investigates each area effectively, you will determine ways to sell the customer that your competition has not thought of. In many cases, these value propositions can be effective enough to unseat a long-standing relationship between a customer and a vendor.

The value scope analysis makes it clear that diversity can be a powerful tool on your team. A sales representative alone would have a much more difficult time gaining access to the information needed to prepare an effective proposal.

Build Value for Your Company Too

Value cuts two ways. Not only must the offering have value to the customer, but the sale must have value to your company. The value scope model measures only value to the customer. It is equally important that the business you are chasing be in alignment with the business your company wants to book. More precisely, will they want to book it in the future, when the customer is ready? We constantly hear sales representatives complaining about all the business they "lost" because their company would not take the order. The problem is that those orders may not have been lost; the salesperson was actually chasing the wrong business.

Most companies aim for a shared set of goals and objectives throughout the entire organization. They communicate their vision statement everywhere—in the annual report, in the newsletter, at every major meeting. CEOs logically expect that their vision will be faithfully carried forward by management and staff. In reality, however, the stated vision is often directly at odds with the activities of the frontline sales teams who interact directly with the customer.

We call this problem *misalignment.* It happens when company policies and practices do not line up with the stated corporate missions. Your team can avoid the serious consequences of misalignment with a little effort. Here is an example of misalignment:

Sprague Electric Company once consisted of a single sales force with two divisions, each with competing missions. The goals of the semiconductor division were shared by the CEO: to develop new technologies and cutting-edge applications of high-margin niche-market devices. The capacitor division, on the other hand, sought to maintain market share with a highly price-sensitive product in a mature market. I went on a sales call with one of Sprague's senior sales representatives who was a top producer with a great deal of product knowledge. As he went through his presentation, it was clear that he was selling very few semiconductors, despite my presence and the company directives. When we got outside, I asked him why. "Steve," he said, "I make an excellent living selling capacitors. The product doesn't take a lot of time to sell and seldom changes. Why should I take time away from my bread and butter just because the company wants to sell more semiconductors?" It made sense to me. But in fact, this talented employee was unintentionally directing the company away from the mission set by the CEO. And he was rewarded for it with large commissions. Not surprisingly, his priorities were shared by most of the sales force.

No wonder Sprague's annual sales projections came up short. There was almost no alignment between the CEO's goals and the sales department's actions. It wasn't simply because the sales representatives had different plans. Corporate management had failed to motivate the sales department to concentrate on the entire product mix. They found value for the customer in the sale of capacitors, but forgot the value their own company needed in the sale of semiconductors.

Sprague continued to pour significant resources inequitably into the semiconductor division. As a result, the two divisions were pitted against each other. Sprague attempted to increase semiconductor sales with countless training programs on sales techniques and product knowledge, but the training was doomed to fail simply because the salespeople could make a better living selling capacitors. The misalignment was devastating to Sprague, causing chaos in the field, missed delivery dates, and frustration among senior managers. Management could not enforce their sales projections on the company because they lacked support from within the ranks. Eventually, possibly as a result of its inability to work as a cohesive unit, the Sprague Electric Company was broken into pieces that were sold off separately.

Align Your Team behind the Company Goals

A company in total alignment has a mission that is coherent and clearly stated. Its strategies, policies, processes, and reward systems are all aligned toward achieving common goals that will have value for the company, the employees, and the customers. Your team should understand these goals and measure your activities against them.

> Align your team's goals with your company's goals and the whole company will support you.

The benefits of total alignment are many, including increased sales, lower costs, higher profits, lower turnover, and satisfied employees. Maybe most important of all, a total alignment company is moved in one direction intentionally by everyone in the organization, as everyday decisions and actions are intrinsically aligned and driven by the same definitions of value.

Here are three steps you can take to ensure that your team's goals are aligned with your company's goals.

1. Include a member of senior management in your planning sessions. It is best if this person has responsibility for areas beyond those of your group. That way this senior manager will be more likely to help you align with the true "big picture."

2. Check regularly with marketing managers of the associated divisions to determine if your sales plans fit with their long-range strategies.

3. Listen for the rumblings of change. If you suspect that there might be a problem, check it out. Sticking your head in the sand is seldom helpful, even for ostriches.

Summary

When value is maximized for all concerned, the sale will close itself. Value works with the natural energy and goals of business and helps all parties realize their ultimate goals. When your team focuses its efforts on understanding and building value for the customer and your company, they will be successful a very high percentage of the time.

7

Team Selling Tactics

Parties who want milk should not seat themselves on a stool in the middle of the field in the hope that the cow will back up to them.

Elbert Hubbard

Sales teams function best when the members are speaking a common language and pulling in a common direction. It is important to be able to communicate to one another where you are in the continuum of work. The sales process described here will be familiar to most experienced sales representatives. This simplified, generic way to look at the sales process is an effective tool for discussing the team selling process. It will help your sales and nonsales team members discuss strategy and tactics from a common point of view.

If you already have a defined sales process, you can easily map the steps discussed in this chapter to your process. If you have not developed a process of your own, I recommend that you start by using the process shown here. As you progress, you will want to customize the steps to fit your company's needs.

The Sales Process (Figure 7-1)

1. Prospect for new opportunities

2. Develop multiple contacts

3. Build an account profile

4. Investigate

5. Make a trial proposal

6. Compile feedback and adjust

7. Propose a solution

8. Deliver on your promises

9. Follow-up

1. Prospect for New Opportunities

Prospecting is the act of finding new opportunities in new or existing accounts. While the initial prospecting of a new account is usually handled exclusively by the field sales representative, teams are very effective at prospecting deeper into an account.

Figure 7-1
The Sales Process

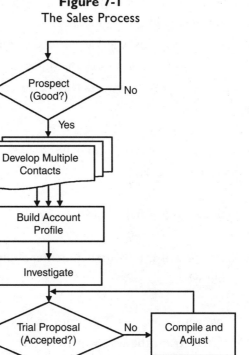

Not only does the team give you more eyes and ears when interacting with the client, but you get the added advantage of the unique perspective that each person brings to the process. In a hospital, a medical expert meeting with a doctor will get different information than a technician from the same team who is meeting with the nurses. By collecting data and comparing notes, they will learn more about who will be involved in the sale and what other opportunities exist for your company than either one could learn separately.

Prospecting is an investigative process that requires constant probing for new information. All members of your team should be asking each of their contacts their own versions of the following questions:

- What problems are you having with your current products or services?

- How could we make your life simpler?

- What pressure is your department under, and how could we help?

- If we were your perfect supplier, how would we be different from the way we are today?

- If we offered the perfect product or service, how would it be different from what you are buying now?

- What do you like and dislike about the competition (or their product or service)?

- What needs do you see in the coming months or years?

- What are your customers requesting?

Your team must constantly be asking these questions to expand their sales opportunities and to stay ahead of the competition.

One of my firm's clients is about to release a new breakthrough product that will literally save thousands of lives. The demand is enormous, and the market is ready to buy. The problem is that the client was late to see the opportunity and their competition will release a version 6 months ahead of their product. That is enough time for the competition to gain market share and earn millions of dollars in added revenue from high prices in a market without competition. That is an opportunity you do not want to miss and an advantage you do not want to hand your competition.

It might be helpful to use an example to illustrate prospecting: A fictitious company named SuperNumbers, Inc. sells Super-Numbers Accounting Software and is attempting to sell their software and services to Soft-Seat Chair, Inc.

Stage One Prospecting

Chris Higgins of SuperNumbers has been scouting the Soft-Seat company for some time now. In her meetings with the CEO and the director of manufacturing, Chris discovered that the company has some problems with their current software. At this point, Soft-Seat is not ready to invest in new software, but they would be willing to let Chris and her team review the system and present a proposal. Soft-Seat figures that the value of the free consulting will be worth more than the hassle it might cause.

Initial Team Creation

Chris has arranged for a team to visit the Soft-Seat head-quarters and tour their manufacturing plant. At this point Chris needs to develop a sales team and prepare them for the first stage of the sales process. Chris, acting as the progress manager, asks for one representative from her accounting systems group, one from the systems consulting group, and one from the manufacturing software group. Her hope is to use these nonaccounting resources to uncover other opportunities and potentially present a more complete solution to the client.

Stage Two Prospecting

Chris has scheduled a meeting at Soft-Seat where she has arranged for the team to meet with key individuals and has scheduled enough time for in-depth discussions. Wisely, Chris has also asked her counterparts in other parts of the world to assist the team by calling on their local Soft-Seat operations and doing an initial prospecting survey. Her experience has taught her that the home office often falls in love with their own choices, even when the results elsewhere are not satisfactory. She hopes that her field resources will bring back issues that her primary team may not hear.

2. Develop Multiple Contacts

As you will see, the order of these steps is often blurred. For example, you will build multiple contacts before, after, and during the prospecting stage. Multiple contacts are critical to sales success for two reasons. First, they give you more information than you could collect from any one source. Second, clients involve many people in the buying process, and by getting to know them, you will have the opportunity to influence them.

Here are five questions to help you identify decision makers:

1. Who else will be involved in this decision?

2. Who was involved in selecting the current vendor?

3. What is (was) your decision-making process?

4. What role does [insert name or title] play in these decisions?

5. Whom does your team turn to for advice on these issues?

Identify the Buyers

We define buyers as all those who have the ability to influence the sale. This is a broad definition, but in today's decentralized companies, it is the most appropriate way to look at the subject. As companies spread out, so does the decision-making process. As a result, the number of people involved in the buying also increases. In addition, it is often difficult to identify the power center in any given buying decision. As a result, a larger number of people must be watched.

We divide buyers into six categories to help us understand their roles and communicate with other team members.

- User

- Functional

- Economic

- Approving

- Friend

- Power player

User. The user buyer actually uses the product or service you are selling. Users care about how it works and ease of use. In a service, they care about the personalities of the people they will be working with. The specialists on the team will often have the greatest opportunity to make contact with users.

Functional. The functional buyer cares about the specifications of the product or service. While these buyers may never actually use it, they will pour over the specifications and ask about every detail. The specialists on your team will usually be the ones who can build rapport with the functional buyer, since functional buyers are often discount salespeople.

Economic.   This person is the key to everything. The economic buyer pays for what your team sells. Economic buyers are usually concerned with the bottom line but are often influenced by the other buyers. The sales professional or senior manager on your team will usually have the greatest chance of building rapport with the economic buyer.

Approving.   The approving buyer signs off on the purchase. While these buyers may not actually have any money, nothing is likely to happen without their signature. Approvers can be interested in any aspect of the sale and must be approached with an open mind.

Friend.   The friend is an important part of your contact list because this person will help you get the sale. Friends want you to succeed and will advise you and give you information to help you. Friends come in two types: those who like you as an individual and those who like your company. Teams have the opportunity of building networks of friends attached to each team member. Be sure to catalog these as you diagram your strategy.

Power player.   The power player has the ability to make the deal happen. Often in a C role, the power player will step in to make things go your way at critical times. Your senior managers and C-level executives can help your team cultivate the power player. There is usually only one involved with each deal.

What You Want to Know about the Decision Makers

When keeping records on people who matter to the sale, you should consider recording two types of information: Information that will help you predict their behavior and information that will help you build rapport with them. For the first category, you should record their educational history, their work background (companies, bosses, teammates), and stories they have told of previous buying experiences. For the second category, you should record birth dates (theirs and their family's), hobbies, past places of residence, political affiliations, and favorite sports teams.

This information can be very valuable in understanding the individual decision maker. It can also be important as new members join the team and need to come up to speed on the client's team.

Ask your team to take a genuine interest in the people they meet when working with a client. While these relationships are intentional and part of the sales process, they need not be disingenuous.

Pairing

In team selling we use a process called *pairing* to maximize the effectiveness of the contacts. In pairing, the team attempts to match each team member with the client contact he or she is most likely to have rapport with. It is not unlike arranging the seating at a formal dinner party. We are looking for pairs of people who will have common interests and backgrounds. At the beginning, keep the pairings as simple as possible. Sales representatives pair with buyers and senior managers. CEOs pair with CEOs, managing directors, and senior vice presidents. Specialists pair with their counterparts in the client's organization.

The goal is for each team member to be seen as a valuable resource to his or her counterpart. By understanding the counterpart's needs and providing valuable advice, each team member will build a connection that will benefit both parties in the end. This is not a manipulative process. Remember, the goal is to help the client improve their bottom line. They can't object to that.

To arrange these introductions, set up a meeting that will require the participation of both teams. We discuss meetings in more detail in Chapter 10, but suffice it to say that very little of this will be left to chance. The stakes are too high, and so are your costs.

3. Build an Account Profile

If the account justifies a team approach, then it justifies an account profile. Every major account should have an account profile since it forms the basis for all other actions to be taken regarding the account. Quite simply, if you don't know what is going on, you can't know what to do.

The account profile contains everything you need to make decisions about the account. Over time, this profile grows and is updated. It must be available to everyone who works on the account. Team members should be very familiar with it, and account representatives must know it by heart. Here are the 15 major components of the account profile and how your team can build one.

1. *Buyers.* Who is involved in the buying process? See "Identify the Buyers" section above.

2. *Organization chart.* This shows who reports to whom. You can often ask for this chart, or a good "friend" will help you create one.

3. *Site map.* Where are the prospect's various plants, offices, and operations located? What is the significance of each location to your strategy?

4. *Contact information.* You'll want to record the complete contact information for every contact that you find. Include, but don't limit yourself to, phone numbers (office, direct, cell, and home), e-mail (personal and business), address, assistant's contact information, and pronunciation of name. The home and administrative information has saved me many times, especially when my contact left the company unexpectedly.

5. *Competition.* Who else has been selling to this account? Your team can ask around and watch the registration book at the client's front desk.

6. *Perceptions.* How does the client perceive your company and the individuals on your team? Are there any misconceptions or bad feelings from a previous experience? Do they like you because of work you did at another account? This information will differ from contact to contact.

7. *Current use.* Which of your company's products or services does the account already use? This can include those used by other divisions too. After all, some of the best referrals come from within the company.

8. *Possible needs.* What needs have you identified at this account? They may be long term or short term. Having a complete list allows you to develop a more effective strategy.

9. *History.* What relationships has your company had with this account in the past? This should include members of your company who have worked for or previously called on the prospect.

10. *Industry.* What industry does this company serve? Where are their products used, and what is their market position within the industry?

11. *Corporate health.* Is the company doing well financially? What do their D&B, P&L, and stock prices look like? Their annual report and SEC reports will give you valuable insight into the health of the company.

12. *Press releases.* Keeping abreast of the company's press releases (see their Web site) can tell you what's new and what they are proud of. Every member of your team should know the latest news about the account. Many free news services will e-mail you when the company is mentioned in the news.

13. *Newsletters.* Most companies publish a regular newsletter for their employees that is packed with news about promotions, new contracts, and awards. Make sure your team has this valuable information.

14. *SWOT analysis.* The classic analysis of strengths, weaknesses, opportunities, and threats always provides a useful look at the situation at hand.

15. *Pairings.* Make sure everyone on your team knows whom you are pairing with whom on the client's team.

4. Investigate

Once you have collected your prospecting data, you need to investigate three qualifying factors:

1. Do you have a viable solution to the problem that is deliverable?

2. Can you show that your product and your prices add up to a positive value proposition for the client?

3. Is this business in alignment with your team and company goals?

If the answer is yes to each of these questions, it is time to develop a value-based proposal for the client. This will take additional investigation and analysis, so organize your team to work together on the task.

> Chris's team returned with great news. Soft-Seat is spending an enormous amount of time and energy transferring information between their manufacturing systems and their accounting software. In addition, their current software leaves the potential for large gaps in the company's financial information. Given new SEC rules on CEO responsibility for corporate accounting accuracy, the team can make a case that the current systems do not ensure that the CEO has accurate and complete data.
>
> An added bonus is that Soft-Seat needs the resources of an outside systems consulting group to address several other issues. They are starting to prepare a request for proposal (RFP) for release next month.
>
> This opportunity clearly passes all three qualifying factors and is ready for a complete value-based analysis and proposal.

5. Make a Trial Proposal

This is another time when teaming gives you an advantage over selling solo. After you have developed a proposal, have your team members check it out with their counterparts. Each may review different sections to ensure that you have understood the needs of the client and satisfied their questions and concerns. The goal is to have no surprises when the formal proposal is presented. In fact, if you are doing this correctly, you will actually be building internal support for you proposal.

Often, the client may not have expected this proposal and may feel the need for a competitive bid. If so, you are in the perfect place to help them write the RFP. That's right; if you have done your job right and the client trusts you, they may actually allow you to define the criteria for the selection of a vendor. Obviously, this gives your team a significant advantage over the competition.

> Chris's team has developed a proposal that includes two new software solutions and a package of consulting services. They have a very good value-based proposal and feel they have solved some of the problems throughout the company.
>
> Chris's team heard from the IT department that the last new software launch was a disaster and the IT department feels that the field operations would fight anything new. As a result, her team will be giving the field operations a first look at the plan to determine if they would support it. The proposal will also be shown to her team's other key contacts for their input.

6. Compile Feedback and Adjust

At this stage, sales teams serve as think tanks and analysts. They compile the feedback from every source they have and develop a plan of action.

Not all information will be given the same weight in the analysis. For example, the needs of the director of information systems will usually be weighted higher than the needs of the assistant plant manager in Sheboygan. However, it is important to remember that there have been situations where an apparently minor player is, in fact, a major decision maker. We look at this issue in more detail in the strategy section of Chapter 10.

The feedback is in from all of the team members and the results are very positive. All the team's counterparts are support-ive of the proposal, even when asked if they would support it with resources from their own budgets. The only reservations are from the operations centers that are short on resources due to a recent layoff and would have a difficult time installing the new software.

There is little value in collecting information if you are not going to use it. Far too often we hear of companies who stared the truth in the face and ignored it. This is the time to put your preconceptions aside and listen intently to the client. It may be your last chance to adjust the proposal before it is formally sub-mitted. The team must keep an open mind, look for creative solutions, and prepare the best proposal possible.

> Chris's team has decided to adjust the proposal to include addi-tional support teams to support the field operations. The goal is to offer them almost a turnkey solution that will require very little effort on their part. This final adjustment to the proposal will over-come one of the last objections and remove any known resistance to the new program. Now the proposal is ready for presenting.

7. Propose a Solution

If you have done your job well, this part of the process may be over before it starts. Since your team has been in close contact with many (hopefully all) of the decision makers during this process, everyone should know what is coming. If you have asked the right questions, you should know how they are going to receive your proposal.

Have you ever noticed that when the President of the United States travels to a foreign country, the press seems to already know what will be decided before the two heads of state even meet? That's because the two heads of state already know! Through their aides, they have worked out the details and come to an agreement that each is comfortable with. There are no surprises, and all that is left to do is smile and use up 25 ceremonial pens. Good business deals work the same way. After all, your team has earned the right to ask the tough questions through their hard work. If you did your job, you should sleep well when the proposal is submitted.

> Chris's team won the contract, and the team celebrated. They took the opportunity to thank everyone involved, including the contacts in both companies. The team arranged a handoff meeting to introduce the team who would be doing the on-site work and to let the customer know that the original team would stay involved. Since the customer had placed their trust in the sales team, they appreciated the continued contact.

8. Deliver on Your Promises

The delivery stage is the beginning of the next sales cycle. Every action your company takes will either add to or subtract from your chances to get the next deal. As a sales team, you must monitor the client's satisfaction with the product or service and give constructive feedback to your operations team.

The delivery stage also gives your team another opportunity to prospect for more business. Even on simple products, you can check on the delivery and ask about other opportunities. On more complex deliveries or service contracts, the operations team is in contact with the client more than anyone else. They should immediately be represented on the sales team and trained to look for new opportunities.

> Chris's team held a transition meeting for the programmers and systems team that would be working with Soft-Seat on the project. Everyone involved was invited to attend. At the meeting, the team laid out what they knew of the client and fielded questions from the project team. When the tactical details were concluded, the sales team asked the project team to do them a favor. They asked them to keep the team apprised of personnel changes and problems that they discover with other software or systems.

9. Follow-Up

Many companies forget the value of follow-up and, hence, miss millions of dollars worth of opportunities. The easiest customer to sell to is the one who has already bought from you. This is especially true if you are there to fix the little problems. At this phase of the sale, the original team may have disbanded and only the service team is left. It is incumbent upon the sales representative and the service staff to work together to identify new opportunities and leverage successes for referrals.

> Chris still stays in touch with the customer service team and follows up directly with the customer after any significant problems. She checks in regularly with contacts to identify new opportunities and to ask for referrals. Last year, when the IT department was recognized for excellence, Chris co-sponsored the awards dinner. To date, this account has spawned a dozen other opportunities for Chris and her company.

Your company must have a defined sales process if you want to get the most out of your sales team. Using the nine steps detailed here, you can build a plan that will keep your company on track to consistent sales success.

Team Ethics

The discussion of tactics is an ideal time to discuss ethics in sales teams. The techniques used in sales can be applied either to the benefit or the detriment of the customer. Everyone on a sales team has an obligation to recognize negative behavior and bring it to the attention of the team. Every organization has its own rules and guidelines for dealing with customers and, at a minimum, you certainly want to obey them. But you might also consider setting your own team standards that supersede other standards. One team's guidelines stated, "When confronted with a decision, we will always do what is in the best interest of the customer."

Take the high road in your sales tactics, and if in doubt, don't do it. If you question an issue, invite mentors, senior managers, and HR professionals to participate in the discussion.

Summary

A sale is a complex process of investigation, strategy, and tactics. While all members of a sales team may not have sales training or sales backgrounds, it is imperative that they each know how the process works and how each member can play his or her role. A well-trained sales team is a powerful force.

8

Tune Up Your Sales Team

*Teams, not individuals, are the fundamental learning unit
in modern organizations. This is where the "rubber stamp meets
the road"; unless teams can learn, the organization cannot learn.*
Peter M. Senge, *The Fifth Discipline*

It's not news that all sales managers want the best from their
team. Fortunately, most team members also want to produce the
best results possible. Peak performance requires proper training
that is based on an evaluation of the team's and individual team
members' needs. In this chapter we will discuss both the evaluation and the training processes and how they can work together
to improve the performance of your sales team.

Evaluate for Excellence

Evaluating the team's selling success is important because you need to ensure that you are getting an acceptable return on investment (ROI). Like all personnel issues, teams are expensive in time, resources, and money. You have the right to demand a corresponding increase in results to compensate you. Effective evaluation is necessary to identify areas needing improvement or "tune-up."

Given that your sales teams are often used to develop long-range customer relationships, revenue alone does not tell the complete story, any more than it would for an individual salesperson. You should establish both quantitative and qualitative metrics, including

- Market share

- Revenue

- Performance against goals

- Customer satisfaction

- Employee morale

- Retention

- Positioning for future sales

- Motivation

- Costs

Not only do these measures give you a sense of the effectiveness of your program, but,

> **Compare results against your defined criteria for success.**

more important, they will give you the tools you need to tune up your sales teams. Just as individuals require feedback and adjustment, so do teams. Without a regular program of evaluation, feedback, and adjustment, your teams will never reach their true potential.

Measuring Results

The most obvious measure of a sales team's success is their sales. Whether you measure it in dollars or units, sales is a clear and simple way to evaluate the output of a team. But as important as sales are, they may tell only a small part of the story.

Team metrics can be both internal (within your company) and external. Some of the traditional internal metrics that should be used to measure team results include

Share of business. Teams should be able to identify and capture a larger share of the available business at a given account due to their additional number of contacts and the diversity in their ranks. When more individuals with unique backgrounds look at an opportunity, they will inevitably see more potential than any one person would see. In order to determine your share of the available business, your team must determine the total market for your products or services at the account. This can be done using either investigations or metrics developed by your marketing department.

Total revenue. While total revenue will probably not increase as a multiple of the number of people on the team, it should increase by more than enough to justify the investment and at a faster rate than it was growing without teams.

Profitability. Teams that are well trained should be able to justify value better than individual sales representatives. Since higher value often yields higher prices, the margins in effective teams should increase. Teams should also have more knowledge and therefore more negotiating leverage to prevent price erosion. One recent study suggests that companies expect new teaming initiatives to return their investment in two years or less.[1]

New opportunities acquired. As part of increasing your company's share of the business at the account, teams must be able to identify and close new opportunities better and faster than the nonteam effort.

One example shows how this can happen. A team from a testing company was visiting a customer to sell them a quality assurance program. While the team's chief engineer was discussing the technical details of the testing program with the director of quality assurance, the VP of operations was working out some minor shipping details with the director of manufacturing. During that discussion, the vendor's vice president asked a simple question: "If we could make this process easier for you, how would we do it?" The answer was surprising. The client suggested that rather than simply testing parts, the testing company could buy the parts, then program, test, and inventory them. Later, as needed, they could ship them in "kits" that were ready to go directly to the manufacturing line.

This new opportunity was completely outside of anything the vendor had forecasted or ever thought of, but it was a profitable opportunity. After some negotiating and a small investment, the testing company began offering this new service to that customer and several others. As it turned out, this new service gave them a strong advantage over their competitors. While their engineers were looking for technical advantages, other members of the team found other opportunities that had even greater benefit to the client. They were able to cement their relationship with the client for many years because of the new service. The quantifiable metrics showed greater sales volume, higher margins, improved customer retention, and lower cost of sales.

Customer retention.   A study by The Yankee Group concludes that fully two-thirds of the customers that leave a company do so because "they feel they have received inadequate care." Obviously, effective teams should offer better service than individuals and "above adequate care." Therefore, it is reasonable to ask your teams to show higher customer retention numbers than you have for nonteamed accounts.

Success against competition.   If knowledge is power, more people with more knowledge should be more powerful against the competition than fewer people. In addition, sales teams have the resources to compile a competitive analysis and strengths, weaknesses, opportunities, and threats (SWOT) analysis on their accounts. This extra effort will yield better results over time. One of the metrics you can use to evaluate your team is how well they fare against specific competitors.

Length of sales cycle.   If the length of your sales cycle is determined by the time required to work through the steps in the sales process outlined in Chapter 7, teams will be highly effective at shortening the time. If the sales cycle is strictly a function of the customer's process, sales teams will have only a marginal advantage primarily due to their ability to circumvent the client's process through their vast network of contacts.

In one sale, a broad-line electronics company was selling transistors to a major radio manufacturer. Over the years, each of the selling company's divisions sold their products separately and in accordance with the rigid process defined by the buyer. That process required each vendor of a particular product to meet at the client's offices on an assigned day. Each was assigned a small room and given a final copy of the request for quote. The buyers would visit each room, review the offer, shake their heads, and move on to the next room. Throughout the day they would systematically beat the best deal out of the vendors.

When the broad-line electronics company switched to team selling, most of the members of the teams from the various divisions told the same story of being powerless in these negotiations. The representative from the custom components division told a much different story. Since their product was unique, they received high margins and no competition. Working together, the team developed a package for the radio manufacturer that included a reasonable percentage of the generic part business in exchange for a small reduction in price on the custom parts. They made the deal contingent on acceptance as a package before the start of the next round of negotiations. The client took it and business increased immediately. This is just one example of how teams have a unique competitive advantage.

Cost of selling. While the initial cost of sales teams can appear significant, effective teams free each other up for other tasks. As a result of this factor and the increased sales they will generate, teams should not increase the cost of selling when taken as a percentage of sales. Sales teams should be responsible for their own budgets for items such as travel and entertainment and rewarded for managing them properly.

Relative to goals. Your teams should also be measured relative to their goals. Goals help focus and motivate teams and using them as a metric reinforces the importance you place on them. Goals are also tied to forecasts and help your company support sales success with appropriate infrastructure. Teams that set and achieve goals help your company in many ways.

> Determine the metrics that will be used to measure your teams and use them effectively.

Customers Know Best

One of the best external metrics for teams is customer feedback. Since team selling is often used as a technique to develop major accounts, improving customer satisfaction is a high priority and a critical evaluation point. Customer satisfaction surveys and interviews can be useful tools to[2]

- Learn where your company stands compared with your competition.

- Track current levels of satisfaction and improvement/ degradation trends before and after team establishment.

- Support team compensation decisions.

- Identify appropriate levels of quality, delivery, and other values that can be critical success factors for your sales teams and company.

- Learn what your current customers, former customers, and prospective customers perceive to be your strengths and weaknesses. This can be used in a gap analysis when compared with the team's findings.

360-Degree Feedback

One of the values of teams can be seen in the power of the 360-degree feedback process. Teams develop a desire for improvement through peer review and support. The 360-degree feedback process provides a tool for assessing the performance of the individuals and the team.

Since this assessment pertains to knowledge, skills, and behaviors as opposed to personality traits, it is an ideal tool for measuring the application of team skills learned in team training.

For the individuals, the 360-degree feedback process breaks through their own perceptions and provides a view of their performance from their peers. Development needs are revealed, and individuals are provided with information that can help them manage their activity in the team as well as in their careers.

For the team, the 360-degree feedback process increases communication between team members and supports teamwork by involving everyone in the developmental process.

Attitude Counts

Studies have shown that teams that believed they were providing better customer service, in fact were. This was confirmed by external surveys, supporting the belief that an analysis of the team's belief in themselves was a valid metric for assessing the team's actual effectiveness.[3] It is therefore important to assess the attitude of the team on a periodic basis.

Behavior Matters

A behavior assessment measures what the team as a unit is actually doing and the quality of their tasks, not their outcomes. This is similar to the periodic assessments many supervisors give employees, except the team as a whole is graded by the leader, manager, or the members of the team in a self-analysis. Behavior assessments help you assess the actions that are the predictors of success.

Position for the Future

In the development of major accounts, positioning for future opportunities is an important goal. The team should be measured on the degree to which they are looking ahead to future products and company initiatives. Customers should have been surveyed on new ideas and feedback provided to the appropriate departments.

> There are many effective qualitative ways to assess team performance.

Team Assessment Form

Rate your team on the following (Figure 8-1):

1. *Commitment.* Your team understands their goals and has agreed to strive to reach them. They are putting in the effort required to accomplish these tasks.

2. *Involvement.* Your team members are taking an active role in the team, including sharing ideas and volunteering for assignments.

3. *Effective communication.*   Communication within the group and between the team, management, and the client is good. There are few "dropped balls" and hidden agendas in the team. Blame is not a factor.

4. *Character.*   Team members respect the responsibility, integrity, dependence, consistency, and discreteness of the other members. There are few complaints about other team members in these areas.

5. *Conflict management.*   The team uses predefined protocols to resolve conflicts quickly, without personal attacks. Few conflicts are escalated to higher levels.

6. *Trust.*   The team members can rely on one another and don't express doubts that assignments left to others will fail.

7. *Establishment of team protocols.*   The team has developed processes for accomplishing their tasks and regularly uses these processes.

8. *Diversity/Role competence.*   Members believe the team is stronger due to the skills, abilities, and knowledge of each of the members. Members regularly call on one another for ideas and assistance.

9. *Problem solving.*   The team is able to identify and solve their own problems through the protocols members have established.

10. *Knowledge bank.*   The team collects, records, compiles, and shares information from a variety of sources.

Figure 8-1
Team Evaluation Form

Category: Quantitative	Goal	Result	Difference
Share of business			
Total revenue			
Profitability			
New opportunities acquired			
Customer retention			
Success against competition			
Length of sales cycle			
Cost of selling			
Relative to goals			
Category: Qualitative			
Commitment			
Involvement			
Effective communications			
Character			
Conflict management			
Trust			
Establishment of team protocols			
Diversity/Role competence			
Problem solving			
Knowledge bank			
Learning			

Team members consistently build and use a database of client information. The database is available to all members.

11. *Learning.* The team actively seeks opportunities to learn and improve the skills of the team and its individual members. Time and resources are allocated for development.

Tuning Up Your Teams

Too many companies abandon efforts like teaming because they do not see results immediately. Team building takes time and effort and requires a learning curve for both the company and the teams. Let's address how you can improve your teams with the information you gathered in the assessments.

Training to Build Teams

The lack of training ranks prominently in the list of top reasons given for poor sales team achievement.[4] The top training needs include management/leadership, team training, and communication skills training. Training needs will differ with the experience of the individuals in the team, but teams provide an excellent opportunity for training because they offer a supportive group setting with regular reinforcement and a defined need.

Important training programs for sales teams include

• Team building

• Communication skills

- Presentation skills

- Team presenting

- Strategic planning

- Effective research techniques

- Leadership skills

- Strategic sales

- Value selling

- Time management

Ways to Improve Training Effectiveness

Unfortunately, less than 10 percent of the money spent on training leads to changes in trainee behavior back on the job.[5] The primary reason for this dismal performance is the lack of an effective training process. An effective training

> **Effective training requires a process, not an event.**

process is a series of six steps that recognize the adult learning process and align the training with it. By following these steps, we can dramatically improve transference or the percentage of skills learned that are actually practiced by the trainee.

1. *Assessment.* Both formal and informal assessments can give your team or team leaders a sense of the training needs. Formal assessments designed to highlight specific areas are often useful to help the team realize

its needs and help the trainer prepare an appropriate training program.

2. *Involvement.* Studies have shown that when you involve the learner in the selection of the training programs, it significantly increases the effectiveness of the learning. While it may be obvious that people who agree to learn are more likely to pay attention, companies too often force training on unwilling employees, only to waste money and hurt morale. Your teams should develop a regular list of desired training for the team and individual members.

   A key piece of trainee involvement is goal setting, which has been proved to increase learning. Your team and your members should set goals for the upcoming training. Teams can later measure the effectiveness of the training and take responsibility for the results. One technique for increasing involvement is giving the team responsibility for the training budget.

3. *Participation.* Adults learn best in relevant, interactive environments. Design your training to involve the team in an activity that helps them learn. Trainers should be familiar with the business and current problems and use this information in the class sessions.

4. *Reflection.* To cement what they have been taught, adult learners need time to reflect on the new skills or concepts and clarify their relevance. Team discussions are the ideal forum for this process. A competent trainer or facilitator can take your group through a series of exercises that will accomplish this goal.

5. *Practice.* New skills move from intentional efforts to habits through practice and repetition. Only 15 percent of skills learned in training remain with trainees one year after training.[6] Much of this dismal lack of success is due to lack of practice. The team environment is an ideal forum for practicing many of the skills required in the field. Communication, presentation, and negotiation skills are easily used within the team's regular activities. A large part of practice is sustaining "share of mind" when other activities are distracting the learners. Newsletters, e-mail, and posters are all effective means for bringing the training back to the top of members' minds and encouraging practice.

6. *Support/follow-up.* Once your teams move into the field with new skills, support becomes critical. In fact, after-training follow-up has been shown to improve learning retention by as much as 37 percent.[7] Teams can designate competent members as resources for those who are struggling with their new skills. Access to trainers or computer-based training programs should be part of every training contract to enable the team to ask questions and tune up their skills once they have had an opportunity to apply them.

Summary

Teams require constant assessment and improvement if they are to be truly effective. It is key to your success to build an atmosphere where personal and group development is an integral part of your goals and regular activities. No higher priority can be found than the development of your people and organization.

9

Tools for Team Success

Progress comes from the intelligent use of experience.

Elbert Hubbard

Your company entrusts its financial life to your sales teams, so it only makes sense for you to give them the tools they need to be successful. If you wanted your race team to win the Indy 500, you would give them more than just the best people. They would get the best engine, the best tires, and the best fuel. If you want your team to win the big sales, they, too, need more than just great people. They need the best information archives, the best knowledge management systems, and the best communications systems.

One of the keys to a team's success is its ability to collect and share information. For this reason, many of the tools described here relate to information or knowledge management and communications. These are the keys to the success of any team selling program.

Knowledge Management

By virtue of their additional contacts with the customer, your teams will collect more information than individual sales professionals. While it is said that knowledge is power, it is only true if the knowledge is recorded and available for others to use in their decision-making processes. Teams without effective knowledge management systems are severely handicapped.

To enable your team to develop a successful selling program, you should

> Build account profiles
> Develop accessible archives
> Compile an expert list
> Provide adequate tools

Build Account Profiles

Every major account should have an account profile. Just like the CIA keeps a dossier on important international figures, your team should keep a file on the account on which you are working. This information will be used regularly to update new team members, prepare for meetings, analyze new situations, and prepare strategies. Here is a list of 12 items that must be in your account profiles:

1. Organizational chart

2. Site listing

3. Contact information

4. Competitive analysis

5. Perceptions chart

6. Current usages

7. Needs analysis

8. Industry background

9. Corporate health analysis

10. Press releases and news

11. Newsletters

12. SWOT analysis

1. Organizational chart. Your team will need an organizational chart of the company or at least the division you are selling to. Organizational charts help you understand how the various players are related and how your team can align to deal with them. They also highlight information you are missing. Have each of your team members ask his or her contacts for an organizational chart, and you will probably have one in a week. Now you can make it accessible and keep it up to date.

2. Site listing.   Many companies operate from more than one site, and it is important to your selling effort that you know where all business is being performed. Much of this information will be available on the company Web site, but many sites only list the major locations. Have someone on the team contact the investor relations department and ask for a copy of the annual report. Most reports list all major company properties and their uses. With the site information, you can match your regional resources with the client sites and learn more about the company and the problems you might be able to solve.

3. Contact information.   You can never have enough contact information. Since you live and die by the people you can get in touch with, you need access to as much information as possible. The Web will have the basic office numbers, but your team needs the works, including e-mail and cell phone numbers. Have each of your team members ask their contacts for a copy of the company directory or phone book. While many companies have rules against giving these out, there is never any harm in asking for it. Nothing gets you past the receptionist faster than a person's direct number!

4. Competitive analysis.   Several members of your team should research the companies you are competing against. You can find them in several ways. First, ask the client; sometimes it's that easy. If not, assume that all of the known competitors will show up or be mentioned so be alert for them in lobbies, sign-in books, and conversations. You can even take the sales representative from your major competitor out to lunch and determine how well he knows your target account. With enough team members asking and looking, there should be very few surprises.

Once you have the names of the competitors, you need to do a competitive analysis so you can find their strengths and weaknesses. Your marketing department should have one. If not, find other teams who have competed with these companies and get all the information they have. You should always call competing companies and ask for a package of information. This will give you the information you want plus a chance for your team members to see how the competition responds to customers. If you need detailed information, have your specialist call their specialist and ask a few questions. Where salespeople and executives will never share what they know, specialists, especially techies, almost always will.

5. Perceptions chart. Very few companies have a neutral reputation. Your team should determine and record the perceptions (Figure 9-1) that each of their contacts has about your company,

Figure 9-1
Perceptions Analysis Chart

Contact Name	Perception of				
	Services	Offerings	People	Prices	Other

individuals, and offerings and the competition's company, individuals, and offerings. Collect this information in a perceptions chart to paint a picture of the atmosphere in which your contacts are living.

6. *Current usages.* Determine what the client is currently using that would compete with your offering. In larger companies you may find that there is not a common solution, leaving you the opportunity to propose one. Once again, teams can collect this information from contacts around the world in very little time.

7. *Needs analysis.* As you do your investigations, catalog all of the possible needs that you see for your offerings at the target account. This ties into the value scope analysis, where each need can be related to a person who is willing to pay for it (see Chapter 6).

8. *Industry background.* What do you know about the client's industry? Is it healthy, growing, downsizing, changing, or evolving? One of the best sources of information is trade magazines. You will usually find the appropriate titles in the client's waiting room. Tear out the subscription card, and you're on your way to the inside track.

One of my clients is in the cruise business. Their sales are affected by the public's desire to travel. Knowing what is happening in the travel industry helps me help my client find new business. Assign someone on the team to be the industry expert, and make him or her responsible for giving the team a regular update.

9. *Corporate health analysis.* How healthy is this company? Do they pay their bills on time? There are several sources of information any team should have. They include the 10K and 10Q reports from the

> You can't build a healthy business on sick clients.

Securities and Exchange Commission, online at www.sec.gov. These annual and quarterly reports can contain sales, forecasts, pending mergers, market problems, legal issues, and more. Buying a Dun & Bradstreet report will tell you about the account's bill-paying habits. If no one on your team understands this area, your CFO or someone from the financial department should be assigned to the team. Not only will this person be able to explain these documents but he or she can train team members to do this analysis for themselves. Teams are a wonderful way to cross-train.

Armed with this information your team can decide if the client is worth chasing or how to adjust the terms of the contract to make a deal possible.

10. Press releases and news. Nothing helps you build rapport with the people in a company better than knowing a little about their current situations. There are two sources to use daily when working with a target account. You can go to their Web site. Many have a section for press releases and update it regularly. Web-watching services like watchthatpage.com are available for free to tell you when a new press release is added. Clipping services are the second option. They are inexpensive and help you compile information from around the world. I use several free ones including Yahoo Events and bizjournals.com that e-mail stories about my clients. They are very powerful tools that keep me on the cutting edge.

11. Newsletters. Company newsletters are full of information that needs to be in your account profile. They are typically

> One or two members of the team can easily monitor the news with the right tools.

published monthly and contain information about new initiatives, promotions, awards, and celebrations. You can pick them up in your client's lobby or you may even be able get on their mailing list.

12. SWOT analysis. Assessing your strengths, weaknesses, opportunities, and threats is an important part of every strategic plan. This analysis will give you a better picture of your competitive situation. The other information collected in the account profile will be needed to perform the SWOT analysis.

Develop Accessible Archives

Your teams will generate volumes of meeting minutes, strategic plans, memos, letters, e-mails, research, and spreadsheets. As new members join the team, they will need access to the history of the team. So will other departments searching for opportunities that others may have missed. Each company should establish an archiving program that is universal across the organization. In this way, everyone in the company will be familiar with the archives and its use will increase. Obviously, an electronic archive is preferable to a physical system since it can be accessed across the company network or intranet.

Compile an Expert List

Knowledge management means the ability for those in need to find those in the know. In most companies, there is an informal network of people with seniority who can point you to the experts you need. This can be an effective way to find your internal resources, but it can be limiting. Many associations have established expert centers to share the knowledge within their ranks. Most are voluntary programs that encourage

> Take time to do the research, and it will pay off in many ways.

members to enter their areas of expertise in a Web-based database. As you find experts, build a shared database for all of your teams to use.

Provide Adequate Tools

Good communications and software tools are essential for effective team selling. An e-mail system with newsgroups and a phone system with conference calling capability are very useful when teams need to exchange ideas, share information, or prepare for meetings. One group I work with has replaced every alternate meeting with a teleconference. The new plan saves time and makes meeting planning much easier.

Telecommunications

Not to forget the telephone, voice mail distribution systems allow those out of the office without e-mail to collect messages and communicate with the team throughout the day. Teleconferencing systems should be easy to use at any time, from any location. Teams need to have the ability to arrange a last-minute conference call from the client's office at 10 a.m. or a hotel room at 10 p.m.

Networking will allow teams to have complete access to up-to-the-minute customer relationship management (CRM) and sales force automation (SFA) information whenever they need it. One study of a pharmaceutical sales application showed such a system returned $100,000 per representative as a result of both access to information and better time utilization.[1]

> Communications systems are critical to the success of sales teams.

Video conferencing and Web-based presentation platforms are making it easier than ever for teams to hold virtual meetings and client presentations. While face-to-face meetings will always build better rapport, virtual meetings allow quicker response time and can include people who might not otherwise be able to attend. A local company uses video conferencing to demonstrate a large machine that would be impossible to take to the client's location. While the virtual approach seldom closes the sale, it often generates enough interest to justify a site visit.

Software

Contact management, CRM, and SFA software are the power tools of team selling. While the lines between these products have been blurred, your team will need the following minimum capabilities:

- Client contact information

- Client organizational chart

- Records of client contacts

- Records of client communications

- Product details and pricing information for all product lines

- Sales history

- Accounts receivable history

- Group mailing and e-mailing

Fully integrated systems automatically record and file all communications that are made with the software. This is clearly the most reliable way to ensure complete traceability.

Team selling may actually be as much a benefit to CRM as CRM is to team selling. In a recent study it was discovered that the major predictors of success in a CRM system were the corporate culture and greater involvement and support at all levels of the company.[2] Team selling is one way in which such systems involve many levels and areas of the company and naturally garner their support.

Project management software has also found a home in team selling. Since selling large projects to large accounts takes time and resource coordination, project management techniques and software are an ideal fit. Gantt charts that show a timeline for all tasks plus deadlines and milestones give a visual representation of the current status and future track of the sales process. Visual tools help facilitate group discussions and make the ramifications of changes more obvious.

Summary

The most expensive part of team selling is the human resource cost. As such, it only makes sense to maximize the team's effectiveness with the proper systems and tools. In addition, many of these systems will allow you to capture the intellectual property, in the form of customer knowledge, that truly belongs to your company.

10

Strategies for Teams

Plans are nothing; planning is everything.
Dwight D. Eisenhower

OK, so you've done the basics. You have scouted out the prospect and determined that they are the right type of company for you to target. They are the right size, they make the right products, they are financially healthy, and there is a good chance that they have an itch you can scratch. Let's face it; you want to win the sale. You can see that contract, and you've already spent the commission! There is only one problem, your customer doesn't care. Yet!

Sales Strategies

Sales strategies are plans that are designed to connect your offering with your client's need in a way that is so compelling that they can't refuse you. In fact, when the strategy is planned and executed properly, the sale should close itself.

It is important to discuss sales strategies in this book for two reasons. First, team selling offers opportunities for sales strategies that may not work as well in a traditional sale configuration. Second, many of the people who will be joining your team do not have a background in sales and therefore need to learn how to plan and implement these strategies. While this will not be an exhaustive discussion of sales strategies, we will discuss specific strategies that can take advantage of a team selling approach.

According to my friend and colleague Dave Stein, author of *How Winners Sell: 21 Proven Strategies to Outsell Your Competition and Win the Big Sale*, you will have the backbone to your strategy when you can complete the following sentence:

The customer will buy from us because_____.

This simple sentence will tell you which product or services to offer, which features to highlight, whom to focus your attention on, and what price to charge. You will also know exactly how to use your team to make the sale. This ties in perfectly with our discussion of value in Chapter 6. The value process will help you uncover the strategic advantages that your team will use to pursue the sale.

> Stay the course unless there is a very good reason to change.

You can already see how this can be an interactive process, can't you? As your team learns more about the client and their needs, your strategy may need to be adjusted to fit the new knowledge. While it is important to be aware of the information around you and flexible enough to react to it, it is equally important to stay focused on your plan and avoid the tendency to engage in a *strategy du jour.*

Don't let your team jump from one plan to another at the first sign of trouble. The leader must look at all the data you are collecting and help the team make decisions that weigh all the facts.

Respect the RFP

It is equally important to avoid being sucked into the RFP vortex. Companies often state, in their requests for proposals, all the areas that are important to them. Unfortunately, RFPs tend to be prepared like stew; everyone dumps something in. It's easy for the committee who is developing the RFP to satisfy many interested parties by adding their favorite item to the list of requirements. In fact, the requirements often contradict each other. As a result, you may get an RFP that is heavy on data and light on information about what is important to the key decision makers. Since committees put RFPs together, teams are needed to take them apart. Your team's job is to uncover who wants what and determine the priority of each item.

A major truck manufacturer received an RFP for snowplows that was impossible to fill. The RFP came from a town in a very snowy part of upstate New York and called for a truck with extremely high horsepower and constant pushing capabilities. Unfortunately, it also specified an automatic transmission, which was guaranteed to overheat with the specified load. The vendors

> Be wary of the request for proposal (RFP).

had to unravel the series of people who had developed the proposal and identify the critical factors. As it turned out, the transmission was a "wish list" item proposed by the drivers.

If your team is seen as a valuable partner and source of information, the client may even ask you to help write the RFP. At a minimum, a good friend should show you the decision-making spreadsheet and the weighing factors they will use to choose a vendor.

Dig In

According to sales strategy expert Neil Rackham,[1] the three best places to start a sale are the focus of receptivity, the focus of dissatisfaction, and the focus of power. The focus of receptivity is the person or persons most likely to listen to you and therefore give you an opportunity to ask questions and explain your offering. The focus of dissatisfaction is the person or persons who perceive problems in an area where you have a potential solution. The focus of power is the person or persons who are in a position to approve, influence, or prevent the sale of your product. The strategies contained in this chapter provide solutions to all three areas.

Start at the Beginning

There are two basic approaches to taking on a large account: chipping in from the edges or going for the central decision makers. Both approaches lend themselves to effective uses of teams, but in very different ways.

Central Approach

I call this the central approach for obvious reasons. In many situations, the central approach is the fastest and most effective approach for selling your product or service.

The central approach is called for when

- Little or no decision making is done at the division level.

- The client's buying process is defined and centralized.

- Your offering's value is best leveraged when sold company-wide.

- You have access to senior decision makers at the corporate level.

It's often easy to believe that the person with the title of buyer at the corporate level is knowledgeable and can make decisions to buy. Any seasoned sales professional knows that both of these assumptions are often wrong. That is not to say that buyers are not smart, but they are seldom experts in all areas. As such, your team has work to do. You must spread out and contact the people who actually need what you sell. Use the value scope model that we discuss in Chapter 6.

Many teams rely too much on the meeting format to gather their information. In these situations, both parties bring together the "relevant parties" to discuss their needs and your offerings. In these public settings, the truth is often protected. Use the techniques in Chapter 6 to help your team members connect with their peers in the client's organization before any meetings are held. I like meetings to be a gathering of people who already know one another. They are better for working out specific issues than for uncovering biases and hidden interests.

In the central approach, your team will be paired with their peers on the client's team. The true power of a team is seen when each member of the team works independently but with a coordinated strategy. In this case, each team member must pursue the following:

- *Determine value.* Each team member's job is to determine the value that his or her counterpart places on various aspects of your offering.

- *Build your case.* Present your offering in a way that supports the strategy statement you defined earlier.

- *Build rapport.* Team members need to build a working rapport with their counterparts. After all, people buy from people they like.

When these pursuits are executed effectively, the individual team members will be able to increase your probability of making the sale by determining your value to the client, validating your strategy statement, and building relationships.

> When you go to the top, bring your best team.

While it is possible for an individual salesperson to accomplish these tasks, teams can do it faster and more effectively.

Another benefit of team selling is clear at this point. The selling company is no longer as vulnerable to the loss of one field person as they were before teaming. With multiple contacts building rapport at many levels, the loss of any one player is less likely to put the sale in jeopardy.

Chipping Approach

You may have discovered that it is sometimes easier to get the attention of the local division of a company than it is to get through to the home office. Chipping away at a company from their divisions or local offices may allow you to get an opportunity to build champions within the divisions who will carry your message to the home office. While many companies use this approach, I find that few make it part of a strategy for selling to the whole company.

Team selling is ideally suited for a successful chipping strategy. By organizing your sales representatives around the country into an effective team, they can call on the prospect's local divisions and then share what they learn. Not only is access often easier to gain through this approach, but you may also discover problems that have not come to the attention of the home office. This gives you additional value points for your eventual corporate sale.

An effective team selling chipping strategy consists of the following steps:

1. Define your ultimate goal. This could be the sale of an enterprise-wide solution to the home office.

2. Determine your strategy, and gain the agreement of the primary sales groups who will be teaming with you. A strategy might sound like this: We believe that XYZ will buy from us because we offer a more cost-effective solution and better service than their current supplier.

3. Lay out your approach. For example: We will contact each of the divisions of XYZ Company independently. We will share the information we learn from these efforts. We will leverage our contacts and successes to allow our major accounts group to sell an enterprise-wide solution to the corporate headquarters.

The best chipping strategies work with the guidance of a team leader or major accounts manager. This major accounts manager acts as your progress manager for the entire global team and communicates with them regularly. I have seen teams that are working on this type of large opportunity hold daily teleconferences to compare notes and adjust tactics. In most cases, effective use of your SFA system or even e-mail can be sufficient.

One client, a major logistics and trucking company, used the chipping strategy very effectively. Since all regional offices were already calling on the local branches of every company in their areas, chipping happened without planning it. On a regular basis, the regional managers would compare notes to determine if there were opportunities worth coordinating. Invariably, the natural overlap of accounts gave them an ideal place to start the chipping process. By coordinating information, they were often able to show the client's independent offices why a corporate-wide agreement was in their best interests. By leveraging this rank-and-file support, the corporate sale was much easier. There is nothing like a testimonial from within the organization to make a sale go easier.

> There is tremendous value in coordinating your individual sales efforts.

Combining Strategies

In reality, the central and the chipping approaches are not separate and unique. As we saw in the trucking company example, the two approaches can be used together to build an effective means of penetrating an account.

Who's Your Opposition?

Every sale is made against one of three groups: the competition, the house, or the status quo. Your strategy will need to address your competition effectively.

Selling against the Competition

The two strongest strategies for selling against the competition are increased value and decreased risk. Your team must know what strategy you are planning to use and how to help you execute it. A client who needs new equipment to support a major manufacturing contract is most likely looking for reduced risk. They already have the contract, so their biggest fear is dropping the ball on delivery. Your strategy should be designed to make all your contacts feel confident that your company is the right partner for them. They will want to hear commitments from your senior management team. Team members should stress reliability and tell stories about successful partnerships in the past.

On the other hand, a client who is fighting with decreasing margins will undoubtedly be looking for value in terms of lower price per performance. Their goal is to improve their output while reducing their costs. Your strategy must be to spread the

> Know your client's needs better than the competition does.

word that your offering has been successful helping other companies in similar situations. They will want to hear case studies and numbers to back up your claims. Team members should be prepared with the required data and ensure that everyone concerned gets the word.

Selling against the House

You are selling against the house when the client has the ability to do the job themselves and indicates a willingness to do so.

Clients may justify doing work internally for one of five reasons:

1. They feel they can do a better job.

2. They believe they can do it cheaper.

3. They have underutilized people they want to put to work.

4. They want to build their reputation.

5. They want to build their kingdom.

While it may be difficult to discern the truth from one person, a team approach will usually determine the underlying motivation by speaking with several contacts and comparing notes. Be sure to brief your team so they know what to look for during their conversations with the client.

The most basic strategy for the first four reasons is to counter with value-based selling. Each member of your team must concentrate on building a case for a greatly improved outcome when your offering is implemented.

Reasons 4 and 5 can often be countered by emphasizing reduced risk. If your offering is seen as the safe way to look good, you will be positioning the client to use you to build their career. Your team should be emphasizing these points with all of their contacts.

Reason 5 is a special case. When it stands by itself, it is often difficult to counter head on. For this reason, having contacts at higher levels is critical. If you are able to make your case to a higher-level influencer, it can often cause uncomfortable questions for the kingdom builder. By preparing the higher-level influencer with the right questions and information, a kingdom builder can become a reputation builder and open to your value-based approach.

> If you know their motivation, you are prepared to make your case.

In each strategy, the power of the team's multiple contacts makes the job of selling the client that much easier. Your team has many opportunities to drop your message into the minds of people who will be in meetings to which you are not invited. The more often your case is argued, the more likely you are to win.

It must be remembered that all people, including buyers, are vulnerable to the opinions of those they trust and respect. Through team selling, you have the opportunity to influence the influencers and build an internal team to fight for your cause.

Selling against the Status Quo

Selling against the status quo means that your client has, or believes they have, the opportunity to do nothing. They think they can continue in their current situation without buying your offering or anyone else's. Your team must show them the error in their thinking.

Even in situations where budgets have been slashed and managers are mandated to operate with the status quo, value selling can be an effective strategy. The key is to find the high-level decision makers and prove to them that your offering will improve their bottom line and give them a large enough return on investment in a short enough time to satisfy their corporate mandates.

If you are a computer wireless networking company selling to a bank with a functioning wired network, you would face such a situation. The bank is doing fine now, and they believe that it is in their best interest to do nothing. Your goal is to show them otherwise. Buried in the bank's budget is a charge for rewiring that must accompany every office move. Your team must work with the appropriate departments to uncover and quantify this cost. In addition, the bank managers have been complaining that they do not have access to the network during their daily briefings. If the managers could connect their laptops during the meeting, they could save about an hour every day and make

> Everyone will buy, once they believe it is in their best interest.

better decisions for the bank. Your team needs to identify the managers who can quantify the value of the wireless network and are willing to be your internal advocates for it. Given enough pressure and justification, you can win against the status quo.

With all of these strategies, you must pair your team with their counterparts on the client side. To identify the people who must be contacted, ask yourself the following questions:

1. Who will be involved in the evaluation, selection, and approval phases of the purchase?

2. Who is ultimately paying for this?

3. Who, on the client side, will benefit from this purchase?

4. Who defines and controls the selection criteria?

Once you have the preliminary answers to these questions you are ready to start. I say "preliminary" because the answers will change several times throughout the buying process. That means you must keep asking those questions over and over.

Summary

Strategic selling provides the organized plan that can multiply the effectiveness of team selling. It is the strategy that allows the team to develop effective tactics and keeps them focused on the real job: making the sale.

11

Successful Team Sales Meetings

Hidden talent counts for nothing.

Nero

For many of you, meetings are the bane of your existence. You waste more time and accomplish less in meetings than any other time of your day. The building of your sales teams is an ideal time to reverse this trend. Effective meetings are an essential part of business communication, and effectively run meetings become even more important as we increase the number of participants as we do in team selling.

Your teams can decide to become meeting experts. When they do, they will accomplish more in less time and find that people are ready and willing to support them. After all, who doesn't want to work on a team where the meetings are short, the requests are clear, and your efforts are appreciated.

In this chapter we discuss internal team meetings, as opposed to client meetings or presentations, which will be covered in Chapter 13. The proper meeting process can be broken down into three steps:

1. Plan for effectiveness

2. Manage for efficiency

3. Follow up for results

Plan for Effectiveness

For many of us, advanced planning means thinking about the meeting in the hallway on the way to the conference room. Let's face it, we're pros and we can wing it. Wrong! Billions of dollars of time and talent are wasted every year attending poorly planned meetings.

One of my old bosses, Phil Pasho, had it right. We were required to have a formal presentation with handouts and over-heads (there was a time before PowerPoint) for every staff meeting. If you did not have your presentation, you could not attend the meeting. At first I thought he was nuts. After all, I was busy and didn't have time for this. The reality was quite different. As a result of our preparation, our staff meetings were shorter, more final decisions were reached, and fewer mistakes were made.

You and your team members have the right to insist on effective meetings. The rules in this section work, so you will get very little resistance to them. In fact, you might find that others appreciate your attention to detail and your commitment to a successful outcome.

In many cases, meeting plans do not need to be highly involved. In fact, you will often find the value of the plan is in the planning process. Simply forcing yourself and others to think through a topic will often uncover valuable information.

Here is a simple planning checklist that you can use as the framework for your planning process. If you post the meeting plan on your intranet for all team members to see, it will allow your team to add their information in one central, shared location. You will note that much of the information will be carried forward from previous meetings and updated.

Meeting Planning Checklist

Goal and Purpose of Meeting

- Commitments to be gained during meeting

- Decisions to be made

- Problems to be solved

- Significant issues to be discussed

Attendee's Information

- List of attendees with name, title, address, fax, phone, e-mail

- How they will attend: live, video, teleconference, written input

Site Information

- Meeting location, directions, start and end time

- Premeeting rendezvous time and location

- Cell phone number to call in case of last-minute problems

Meeting Details

- Agenda: roles, subjects to be covered, order of events, and time allotted for each topic

- Equipment required (presentation and demonstration), person responsible, arrangements confirmed

- Information to be gathered—any information required for the meeting and who is responsible for collecting it

Postmeeting Responsibilities

- Follow-up on commitments, person responsible

- Minutes distributed, person responsible

Invite the Right People

Two types of people need to attend your meetings:

1. Those who are going to do the work

2. Those who are going to influence or approve it

My preference is to allow those who are not affected by a particular meeting to skip it. They are always welcome to sit in and listen, but most people have other places to be and more important things to do than sit in a meeting that is not relevant to their jobs.

Get Senior Managers to Attend

The most difficult groups of people to attract to meetings seem to be senior managers and corporate officers. I have attended too many meetings where the vice president was critical to the outcome of a decision and was missing in action without any notice. These busy people skip meetings for one reason: They believe that the meeting can go on without them. In other words, they trust you to make the decisions. Unfortunately, there is a limit to your authority, and sometimes you just need them there.

Here is a foolproof way to ensure that you will never waste time waiting for key players:

1. Don't include them in the standard e-mail meeting blast.

2. Send them a special invitation that says the following: We are having a meeting next Thursday at 2 p.m. to decide [insert topic]. I believe that your input on this decision is critical. If you cannot attend, please let me know so that we can reschedule the meeting. While they may not attend, you will certainly hear back and avoid wasting your time.

Send the Agenda in Advance

The key here is for you to have the right people with the right information prepared and ready to go on time. The agenda is

Agendas are critical to the success of your meetings.

the road map for the meeting, telling participants what they will do, when, and how long it will take. Without a map, there is little chance you will end up where you intended to go. Without an agenda, there is little chance you will cover the material you intended in the time you allotted.

Agendas also allow the participants to see what will be discussed and to think through what they want to contribute. We know from studies of learning styles that over 25 percent of the population are uncomfortable being asked to respond with off-the-cuff remarks. They would prefer to give an answer after having had time to contemplate the issues. Have you ever noticed that some of your brightest team members do not contribute in meetings, but they send memos or start one-on-one discussions in the hall afterward? If these same people were prepared for the meeting, many of them would have argued fiercely for their positions. Unfortunately, the people who tend to run meetings have exactly the opposite style, and they love shooting from the hip. Without an agenda, you lose out on the contributions of an important sector of your team. Send participants an agenda with ample time for them to look into the critical issues and your meetings will be full of contributors.

Manage for Efficiency

Meetings seldom run well without the proper management. On top of good planning, it takes a good set of rules and a team willing to follow them to make a successful meeting. We will look at the beginning, body, and end of meetings to find some simple ways to make them work for you and your team.

Start the Meeting Right

Start your meetings with a brief overview. It should not be anything big and formal. If every meeting starts with a commitment to the rules, the agenda, and the end time, your team will take these preconditions more seriously.

- Review goals and agenda

- Set ground rules

- Review end time

Keep Participation Even

Don't let a few people dominate a discussion. Work with the group to ensure that everyone is heard. Dominant team members may overshadow others who have equally important information. To accomplish equal participation, use methods that ensure that all ideas are heard. For example, professional trainers and facilitators seldom ask for a show of hands during brainstorming sessions. Instead, they use a variety of small-group techniques to elicit information from all members of the group. In any group, some people will always raise their hands and some never will. Allow for everyone's participation by breaking into small groups to collect ideas that can be reported later to the whole group.

Dealing with Naysayers

Convert negativism into positive ideas. On occasion, teams have a negative member or guest. When you hear "That won't work," try the "Help us understand" technique. Ask the person to give you every reason he or she can think of for the idea's not working. Now ask the participant for suggestions for changes that might make it successful. Document all of these ideas on a flip-chart and thank the participant for his or her help. You have just turned whining into data, which is almost alchemy.

Manage Time

Meetings tend to define the work that will be done after the meeting. Therefore, it is very important to get your team out of the meeting on time or early by sticking to the agenda. This requires that the meeting facilitator get permission from the team to cut people off when their time is over. The permission gives the facilitator the power to summarize long-winded speakers, park off-topic subjects, and stop interruptions and side conversations. Take control and your team will appreciate it.

Since an agenda was worked out in advance and time allocated for each topic, you must decide how to handle topics that run over their allocated time. There are two things to remember:

1. Your team must get the important work done.

2. You must finish on time.

These two rules often seem to conflict until you remember that it's the important work that must be accomplished, not all the work. When time gets short, your team must prioritize the items that must be addressed by the group now.

My favorite option is to ask how many participants want to discuss a particular issue now. If over half the room wants to go on, you'll have to agree to either extend the meeting or cut another topic. If it's less than half, ask the group that is interested to arrange a time after the meeting for further discussion.

Stay on Track

Another problem arises when members of your team get off the subject. When this happens, the person with the new idea may want to discuss it immediately. Your job is to keep the meeting on track while assuring your team member that his or her idea will get a fair hearing at the appropriate time. The traditional "parking lot" works best here. One piece of flip-chart paper or note pad is reserved for subjects that arise but are not on the agenda. Each one is placed on the list and tabled until near the end of the meeting. At that time, the list is reviewed and each item is placed in one of three categories:

1. Referred to someone for study or action

2. Placed on the next meeting's agenda

3. Scratched off and ignored

The team should work together to make these decisions.

Record Minutes

As the meeting comes to a close, your team should decide on their next steps and action items. Each should be assigned to a specific individual with a definite date for completion. These assignments and dates form one section of the meeting's minutes. The minutes should include the following:

1. Date, location, and list of attendees

2. Brief description of presentations given and where copies can be obtained

3. Brief description of decisions made

4. Brief description of the topics discussed

5. Next steps and responsibilities

6. Action items assigned, to whom, with committed completion dates

Wrap It Up

Meetings are either effective tools to move actions forward or black holes that suck the same issues back in over and over again. To end the black-hole syndrome, end your meetings in a way that ensures that actions will be taken.

> Run your meeting properly, and you'll find everyone is willing to attend your sessions.

Recap the results, and walk through the action items and next steps. Ensure that one responsible party has taken ownership for the completion of each action item and that this information is recorded in the meeting's minutes.

- Recap outcome

- Assign action items

- Define next step

- Review quality of meeting

- Schedule next meeting

Follow Up for Results

Since participants will go back to work to find full in-boxes, voice mails, and e-mails, it is important to remind them to follow through on their commitments. Done correctly, they will appreciate your professionalism.

> Following up on meeting responsibilities will avoid costly and embarrassing problems in the future.

The follow-up can be the responsibility of the leader or anyone he or she designates. Following up is simply a way of keeping the team on track and ensuring that everyone is giving it the attention it deserves.

1. The minutes must go out via e-mail immediately after the meeting.

2. Record follow-up dates for action items in your calendar for future reminders.

3. Follow up via e-mail or telephone well in advance of the deadline.

Summary

Effective meetings are critical to the success of any sales team. If the team develops an effective meeting protocol, they will accomplish more in less time and with much less stress. The time spent perfecting your meeting style will be well invested.

12

Build a Team Culture

Culture is to a group what personality is to an individual.

Cornelius Grove

If your company has used a more traditional selling style, team selling may feel like an unnatural process. Many of the structures and habits that support your traditional system will hurt the chances of success with team selling. Compensation plans, forecasting processes, management structures, attitudes, and even computer systems may detract from the effectiveness of this new way of operating. To increase the likelihood of success in team selling, your management team must make the decision to change to a team selling culture, not just team selling tactics.

Establish Your Core Values

Many companies have mission and value statements, but not all of them live those words. To establish a team selling culture, you must establish team values that work and live them.

Values define what is important to you. Figure 12-1 shows examples of different value choices that may be made by your company that affect sales teams.[1]

> Core values define many of the decisions and actions taken by the team.

Differing opinions over values are natural and healthy for teams if they are included as part of the team development process. Teams that are involved in setting their values will tend to support and defend those values more than if the values were defined externally to the team.

Figure 12-1
Value Choices That Affect Teams

Value Choice A	Value Choice B
Technical considerations are critical	Relationships and trust are critical
Leaders should be "in the know" and in command	Leaders should collaborate and motivate
Deadlines must be made at all costs	Deadlines are guidelines to measure performance
Communication should stress accuracy	Communication should stress harmony
Quality is our number one goal	Making the monthly numbers is our number one goal
Teams should make their own decisions	Everything should be done right the first time
Team harmony and unity are highly valued	In tough situations, senior managers know best

Define Your Way

From the time we are young children, we learn that people expect and respect rules and order. For a group of people to function effectively, they must have an expectation for the way things will happen. These expectations are called *protocols.*

Protocols define a wide range of group behaviors and activities including meeting rules, performance appraisals, and reprimands. They contain a set of norms for handling the day-to-day activities of communications, task assignments, and group interaction. Protocols can also cover dos and don'ts of cultural issues, behaviors, and client treatment. Protocols often develop from the resolution of a problem. For example, if the team tends to isolate new members, they may decide on a protocol that says "new members speak first at all meetings" for three months. If sensitive e-mail is often misinterpreted, the team may decide that sensitive issues will be handled on the telephone. Protocols are a way of preventing problems. They can also be the lasting bridge that is left behind after the effective resolution of a problem.

Here are some sample protocols:

- When making requests, we will supply the background and reason for the priority. "ASAP" and "Urgent" will be reserved for true emergencies.

- Team leaders and managers will not be assumed to be correct or to have the answers. We will challenge them using our best ideas.

- Only the timekeeper will be allowed to interrupt a speaker during a meeting. We will listen to all ideas in full.

> Protocols clarify acceptable team behavior.

Teams should build their own set of protocols as the team grows and develops. They may want to share them with other teams and explore how others have handled similar situations. Leaders and managers should encourage the establishment of protocols as a means of turning a specific conflict resolution into a general team improvement project.

Develop Trust

One of the most valued commodities in human relationships is trust. In teams, trust is the key to individuals supporting one another and an essential prerequisite for open communication. Trust has also been shown to affect how individuals view one another's performance. Trusting groups perceive themselves to have a greater degree of success than nontrusting groups. For these reasons, it is imperative that your company and teams develop an atmosphere of trust.

Trust is earned by one party investing time, effort, and other irrecoverable resources in the relationship. In other words, when companies show that they support the team concept through compensation, training, and resource commitments, teams begin to trust the organization. Individuals accomplish the same trust building when they offer closely held information, such as key contacts, and are willing to make time to attend meetings to help other members of the team.

Clear, common goals are another way to instill trust in teams. When everyone perceives the others as working toward the same end, friction is reduced and trust is supported. Joint training, role playing, and team exercises are effective techniques for building trust.

> Trust in the team and the organization is critical to the success of any sales team.

Trust in the team translates to the client as a more effective selling organization. Partners who trust one another are more likely to work independently. Team members who trust one another are also more likely to speak well of the others in the group and thereby instill trust in the client.

Encourage Learning

The need for learning is highest when change is the greatest. Those promoting the change must learn to identify and capture the best of their creation, while those undergoing the change must learn to manage and take advantage of it. Sales teams are on both sides of this equation at the same time. It is therefore imperative that they be provided with the learning opportunities they need to succeed.

In a survey of attendees at the Strategic Account Management Association Conference in May 2001, one of the top obstacles to achieving success was insufficient team training. Companies should allow the teams to budget their own training, with the support of the training and human

> Learning is essential to mastering change. It must be encouraged in the sales team.

resources departments. Programs teaching skills such as leadership and management should be open to all members, recognizing that each member will lead over the course of the sales cycle.

Define Effective Compensation Plans

One of the most sensitive areas of team selling is compensation. In many companies, this is the first time that employees without "sales" in their titles will be paid for what they produce. This concept is difficult for both the sales and nonsales personnel. Companies switching to team selling need to address two questions:

1. How will you reward all players equitably and fairly?

2. How do you ensure that your top performers, who thrive on large commissions and competition, continue to be motivated to perform under the new pay plan?

These are not trivial questions, but they have answers that can result in greater rewards for all involved.

To begin with, you must clearly define your goals. Decide if you want to achieve fairness or equality? Decide if you want to use money as the primary motivator or if you believe you can motivate in other ways.

If you want to motivate with money, what metrics do you want to tie compensation to: dollars, units, profit, customer retention, new business, specific types of business, or a combination of several factors?

Whatever you choose, there will be repercussions. Sales will typically want more. Some groups may fight commission all together. One unionized group refused bonuses because the bonuses were tied to performance and they feared the effects of differentiating the individual's worth.

Everyone must recognize the value of all team members to the ultimate mission. Obviously, the salespeople are important. But when orders are backed up, manufacturing clearly plays a critical role. When special requests arrive, engineering may be the most important group. You may want to reward these groups for their performance.

In the initial move to sales teams, many companies experience a drop in sales and an increase in margins. This is due to the longer sales cycle for bigger sales and the fact that you are selling higher in the organization and adding more value to the sale.

Most companies find that their plans evolve. The *Times* newspaper in Munster, Indiana, started with a unique plan that made everyone a free agent. It was called *consenting adults* because no one was forced to work with anyone else. They allowed sales reps to build their own teams by paying graphic artists part of their commission as a reward for joining their team. This plan helped build the teams but served its usefulness after a year or so. They currently commission all members of the teams on sales and growth.

Consider these factors in your compensation planning:

Fears of Salespeople

- The sales staff may feel that they deserve a bigger share of the pie.

- They may not be willing to give up their higher commission percentages.

- They may fear that the nonsale group will be "slackers" and not carry their weight.

Fears of the Non-Salespeople

- They may be uncomfortable being measured by results that they do not completely control.

- They may not be comfortable with the risk involved.

- They may feel that others on the team will not work as hard as they do.

Benefits of Team Compensation

- Team rewards motivate people to support one another.

- Teams sell more; so lower percentages can still yield increased dollars.

Options

- Team rewarded on percentage of quota

- Team rewarded on sales growth

- Team rewarded on profitability

- Team splits bonus evenly

- Team gets same percentage increase of base salaries which are different

- A commission system for sales and a point system for the nonsale bonuses

- Straight salary

When John Sample, CEO of Business Interiors, shifted his company from a "lone ranger" approach to a team-based organization, one of the scariest aspects was figuring out the compensation system for the sales force. He spent a lot of time pondering what was fair.

To get some answers that everyone could accept, the company conducted a wage-and-salary survey, which has become an annual event for the office furniture dealership in Irving, Texas. Mr. Sample asked his sales teams to submit proposals on the type and level of

> Compensation plans generate sensitive issues that demand the utmost attention.

compensation they'd like to be paid. CEO Sample stated, "We weren't far apart when we finally did that. It was really one of the smallest problems when I got down to it." He proceeded to develop a system that included individual incentives for salespeople out calling on customers and rewards for the entire sales team when certain profitability levels were reached.

Summary

Teams do not exist in a vacuum. They live within your company and are affected by all aspects of the larger organization. As you implement teams, examine your culture and make the necessary adjustments.

13

Client Meetings and Presentations

A sale is not something you pursue; it's what happens to you while you are immersed in serving your customer.

Author unknown

We all know how the standard team sales client meeting is planned. You try to get the key players to show, but the dates that are good for the client are bad for your best players. So you take the second string and try to make the best of it. Advance briefings consist of a few e-mails to tell the team where you will meet them at the airport and then a rendezvous with the team at McDonald's around the corner from the client's office 15 minutes before the big meeting is to start.

If you were to request thousands of dollars of company money for a special event, you would have to jump through hoops and would probably be turned down. On the other hand,

> Client meetings are expensive and important to the sale. Plan accordingly.

you can commit the company to spending an equal amount in travel and lost time by flying a team to Dubuque, Iowa, and no one bats an eyelash. If team selling is to be successful in your company, the costs have to be managed in the field by increasing the value of client meetings.

In this chapter, we will discuss how the power of teams is multiplied when used effectively in client meetings and presentations. This is the high-wire act for teams, because it exposes their coordination skills to the client. Today's clients measure the quality of your offering by the competence of your team. If you look like the Keystone Cops, you'll lose. But if you look like the Bolshoi Ballet (skip the tutus), you'll gain serious points in the client's eyes.

Planning for Effective Meetings

Like any meeting, the planning starts with a clear definition of the goals and expectations. Both sides need to know what to expect from the other and what is expected of them. If I had a nickel for every time I heard a client say, "I thought you were going to discuss X" or "We don't need to hear about that," I'd have toll money for a lifetime.

The key to effective meeting planning is the same as the key to effective sales: questions. The more you understand about the client's needs and the interests of the people who will be attending the meeting, the more likely you are to succeed. It's important to remember that the various players have differing goals. The buyer might simply need

> Determine the client's goals before planning the meeting.

to bring a solution to the table. His biggest fear is that the meeting will be off topic or boring. He wants to end the meeting with his operations staff patting him on the back for finding a great resource for them. On the other hand, their engineer wants an answer to her problems and needs detailed information. The department manager is afraid you'll dangle a great technical solution in front of the engineer, but you'll fall down on the implementation. Don't be afraid to ask questions before the meeting is planned. Be terrified of sitting in a meeting full of people who want answers to questions you don't understand.

Include the Right People

As part of the planning process, you should have identified the decision makers in the client's organization and documented their needs and interests. It is key that you have in attendance as part of your team people who can adequately address each of the decision makers' interests and needs. You can also bring as part of your team those people whose counterparts you have not been able to gain access to. This is a great opportunity to get beyond the 'buyer' and reach those who are involved in all aspects of the decision. If you are bringing your software interface designer, the client is obligated to have the person responsible for the interface in attendance. You can also confirm this in advance to ensure that the right people from each side will be attending.

Another way to pick the "right people" is to match the personalities of the client's

> The right team makes a more effective meeting.

team with your team. Pick people who will get along, especially if there are individuals on the client's team who you do not particularly hit it off with. You may be facing a problem with one of the buyers, while another member of your team may be able to hit if off famously with that person. I can remember many situations where buyers or other client personnel asked me to bring so-and-so along next time. I tried not to take this as an affront to me personally but as an opportunity to make a deeper connection with the client.

Handle the Invitations Correctly

One easy way to ensure that the right people will attend is to handle the invitations yourself. Tell the client that you have packages of information to send to the participants to make the meeting more effective. If

> When you handle the invitations right, the right people show up.

they will give you the contact information, you will see that each participant all gets the information that pertains to his or her area of interest. You might even have their counterparts on your team call or e-mail them to introduce themselves. If they do, the first meeting will seem more like a warm reunion than a cold introduction.

Pull Out the Big Guns

This deeper connection is never more important than when you are attempting to sell at a higher level in the organization. If you need to make a connection with the client's CEO or a division director, one tried-and-true approach is to bring your

CEO or senior vice president along to the meeting. This gives you the right to ask to

> **Big guns bring out big guns.**

have their counterpart attend the meeting too. Be sure to get their commitment in advance, since this approach can backfire when your CEO gets stood up by theirs.

Alternatives to Live Meetings

An alternative to bringing the right people along is to have them on the phone or video conference. This can be a very effective approach that presents you as a resource to the client. Speakerphones can be used in conjunction with a slide presentation or a Web-based presentation. This gives the client access to the expert while you manage costs and schedules.

An effective technique is to ask several of your resources to be standing by their phones at a particular time, just in case you need them. If the client asks a question that pertains to your expert, ask for permission to get your expert on the phone. You can make the introductions and facilitate the discussion. I helped a client arrange a series of presentations around the country when the cost of dragging the entire team with us could not be justified. The teleconference alternative was well-received in every situation.

> **You don't always have to fly in to have an effective meeting.**

Video conferencing can also be effective if the client has the appropriate equipment. The visual media gives you the opportunity to build more rapport than audio alone, and it also provides a chance for product demonstrations.

Running Effective Meetings

Your leader should open the meeting with introductions and an overview of the agenda. Take this opportunity to ask if there are any changes to the agenda needed and get the client's approval to proceed. Your leader should be the person that you want the client to see as their main point of contact. By facilitating the meeting, your leader is strengthening his or her position.

Introductions should include name, title, and reason for being at the meeting. For example, one person might say, "I am Judy Nesbit, I am the director of marketing at Very-Good Software, and I am here today to listen to your current and future needs. Another might say, "I am Bill Williamson, I am with Very-Good's technical support department, and I am here to address your problems with the current version of our software."

While exchanging business cards is common practice, it is very polite for each group to present a list of attendees containing name, title, phone number, and e-mail address. This list should be distributed before the introductions to allow for note taking. If people are trying to remember names and titles, they will not be concentrating on the topic at hand. Since we know that most people are poor at remembering names, these lists put everyone at ease.

> Be sure to get everyone's contact information.

Work as a Team

Even in a two-person team, you should always decide who will be the "lead" and who will be "support" before you meet with the client. The lead should control the flow of the conversation and bring the support person in as appropriate. This may mean that the support person does most of the presentation and the leader facilitates the discussion. Whatever the case, a decision in advance will improve the flow of the meeting and give the client a feeling of confidence in a well-organized team. Never fight for time or the "last word" in front of the client.

> **Plan your teamwork.**

Work for your teammates. If one of your presenters has handouts or presentation materials, make sure someone else is prepared to hand them out. Assign one person as gofer in case the speaker needs something during the program. This allows your presenter to remain focused on the client, and it also shows the client that you are working as a team to support them.

The Listener Controls the Room

In team meetings, the listeners on your team control the client's eyes. If the person listening looks at the client, the client will return the look and be distracted from the speaker. If listeners look at the speaker, the client will also focus attention on the speaker. Listeners should look at the speaker and pay attention. If team members look focused and interested, everyone will be focused and interested.

> **The listener controls the client's attention.**

Handle Time Problems Quickly

On occasion, you will have people who talk longer than the time allotted on the agenda. Here are a few client-friendly approaches to dealing with those who are running over the allotted time. It is best if each leader is prepared to handle his or her own side, but done correctly, any team member should be able to make one of these suggestions.

> You should control the flow of the meeting.

1. Cut the person off if both sides have agreed in advance that this is appropriate.

2. Ask the speaker whether he or she can summarize and conclude in three minutes.

3. Ask the group if this topic demands more time in a whole-group session or if it can be deferred to a subgroup.

4. Ask if documentation could be provided to explain this point so the group could review it before the next meeting.

Remember that time can work against you in your meetings, so schedule the critical items early in the agenda.

The Power of Small Groups

The power of your team can be seen when members have time to meet one-on-one with their peers. You can schedule time, after the meeting, for the various peer groups to meet separately. This is the time for deep technical discussions that would drag down the general meeting. Note that many technical types prefer a one-on-one discussion to a large presentation and will give

you much more candid information in this setting.

> Peer-to-peer meetings build rapport and unlock valuable information.

Peer-to-peer conferences
allow for a depth of discussion
that would not be practical in the group setting. They allow for deeper rapport building and provide an opportunity to ask questions that could be embarrassing for the client to answer in front of their team. More can often be accomplished with three or four short, parallel meetings than in one long group meeting.

It may be effective to bring the entire group back together for a wrap-up meeting following the peer-to-peer conferences. This gives all the groups a chance to summarize their findings and present their next steps. In any case, it will be critical to debrief your team and capture both the action items for the minutes and their insights for your private files.

Wrapping It Up

As the meeting ends, it is once again time for your leader to take the helm. The leader should revisit the goals and determine if they were met. The leader should collect a list of open questions or requests for information that must be completed after the meeting. Each team member should have been collecting these items throughout the group and peer meetings and, if possible, presented them to the leader before the summation.

> The last commitments of the meeting are often the most important.

The key players need to agree on the next steps and how they will be handled.

Leave the client with one clear point of contact. When you end the session, let the client know whom they should contact. In some cases there are different contacts for different situations.

Clarify this by offering one person as the primary contact for any questions. In large presentations, a list of your contact people and their responsibilities should be prepared in advance and offered to the client.

Debrief Your Team

I once met a very successful businessman who had built several businesses and sold them off for handsome profits. When I asked him his secret to success, he said simply, "I know how to finish the things I start." In selling, many doors are opened and few turn into sales. We call this our closing ratio, but in many cases it is actually our follow-through ratio. After you spend the time to plan, rehearse, and put on an effective team selling presentation, take a few minutes with the team before everyone scatters and debrief. Here is a checklist of items to cover:

- How did we do compared with our plan?

- What should we do better next time?

- What did we do well that we want to repeat?

- What did we learn about the client and their needs?

- What promises were made?

- Who is going to follow up? By when?

- What is our next step?

Record the postmeeting information while it is fresh in
everyone's mind and get the
minutes and action items dis-

> Don't leave the valuable information in your team members' heads.

tributed immediately. One way to get more support from the
rest of your team is to make their action items clear by writing
them down.

Team Sales Presentations

Sales presentations are the most complex of meeting environments. They often involve a larger, more diverse group of
people than the traditional solo sales presentation. The very nature
of the team sale means that multiple products and services
are likely to be presented as an integrated package to a client
whose buying process may actually be less integrated than your
selling process. While your team may have done considerable
work with members of the client organization to get to this
point, many buying decisions are actually made as a direct result
of the formal presentation. This is an opportunity for all the
members of the buying team to see all the members of the selling
team. If they like what they see and hear, the sale may be yours.

Buyers buy for many reasons and all of them must be covered in the major presentation. First, buyers buy because your
offer is to their advantage in one or more ways. Second, they buy
because they believe your company has the ability to do the job.
Third, they buy because they believe that your company has
either the best chance of success or the least chance of failure.
Fourth, they buy because they think that you and your team
will be easy and enjoyable to work with. You can sum it up

in four words that must be represented in every sales presentation: value, competence, confidence, and congeniality. In this section, we look at ways to ensure that your team succeeds at all four.

The typical team sales presentation is characterized by a group of four or five canned presentations, loosely tied together by a sales representative who has only a vague idea of what is to be presented. As a result, the probability of success is low and the costs in terms of resources used and opportunities lost are enormous. Your team may actually be doing much better, and for that I applaud you. But this is the time for taking things to a higher level, so let's take the presentation process apart and find out what makes it work. Our goal should be an effective, repeatable process that your team enjoys.

Have a Clear Message

Every presentation needs to have a simple, clear message that you hope to deliver to the client. You should be able to state it in one or two sentences that everyone on your team understands. Refer back to Chapter 10 and the discussion of Dave Stein's strategy statement that says you must be able to complete the statement, "The customer will buy from us because _____." The test is to be able to answer yes to this question: If the client already believed your message, would they sign the agreement? Here are two examples we can work with.

> *Example 1:* By working with Alpha Group, our prospect, OneCo, would have the best opportunity to exceed their goals over the next 12 months and do it with minimum risk.

> *Example 2:* After buying and installing equipment from
> Beta Engineering, Unified Manufacturing will have
> reduced manufacturing costs by 10 percent, lowered
> downtime by 12 percent, and achieved an ROI recovery
> of 10 months, 8 months shorter than the competition.

Notice that once you have the message defined, you have
the objectives for the presentation too. In the first example,
Alpha Group must first show how they can help OneCo exceed
their goals within the next 12 months. Next, they must assure
them that there is minimal
risk in the product or service
and in working with Alpha
Group. Cover both of these

> One clear message is easier
> for the client to understand.

bases and you have significantly increased your odds of success.
In the second example, Beta Engineering must first make their
case that they can reduce United Manufacturing's manufacturing
costs by 10 percent. Next they must show how they can reduce
downtime by 12 percent. Finally, they must show that United
Manufacturing will get a return on investment that will cover
their cost of purchase in 10 months. Each objective is a separate,
distinct, specific promise that must be supported to a high enough
degree that the buyers are willing to stake their jobs on it. If
you miss one piece of the puzzle or even just come close, you
open the opportunity for your competition to steal the business.

Pick the Right Team

When producers decide to finance a play on Broadway, they
spend countless hours looking for just the right person to play
each unique role. That's because, no matter how good the script
or how famous the writer, the presentation comes alive through

what the audience sees on stage. You just can't have a King, in *The King and I*, who does not exude confidence and power. You must pick people to present who, in the eyes of the specific buyer, embody the message you intend to send.

If you need to show credibility in a technical area to the client's technical buyer, bring an engineer. Could the marketing manager, who was an engineer 10 years ago, do the job? Not if you want the client's engineers to believe the story. The same goes for corporate commitments. If you are promising a complicated delivery schedule, you need someone on your team who controls operations to speak with credibility to their operations buyer.

Let's look at our examples. In the first group, you will need someone who speaks the customer's language and knows their business. You may also need a senior executive to make the commitments necessary for the prospect to take the gamble with your company. In the second example, you clearly need a manufacturing expert backed up with a financial expert to support the claims you are making.

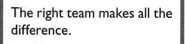

The right team makes all the difference.

The next question is, How many people do you need? I recommend you bring just the number you need. While some suggest you should bring sufficient numbers to dominate the room, I disagree. I have seen two or three talented people sell a buying group of twenty, and I have seen twenty sell to a group of three. Ask yourself if adding that next person will help the client answer yes to your original question. If not, leave that person home.

Practice Makes Perfect

Are you good at winging it? Can you stand up and get the meeting going without any preparation? Some of you can and that's why you do. Unfortunately, the people you bring into the field may not know the account as well as you do and are likely to say the wrong thing at the wrong time. Every sports team has a planning session to discuss every opponent every week. Even though they know the other team very well and have played them before, they still take valuable time to go over the unique aspects of this opponent and to ensure they all know how they are planning to approach each situation.

While I don't want us to look at our clients as opponents, the analogy holds a great lesson for sales teams. Get your game plan together, and make sure that everyone knows what to do. A premeeting rehearsal can be handled on a conference call a few days before the meeting. Here is a list of the items you might want to include in your premeeting rehearsal:

- Agenda

- What must be covered

- What must be avoided

- Potential problem areas

- The client's expectations

- Information you want your team to try to collect from the client

- Information you want to avoid telling the client

- Answers to the questions you hope you are not asked

- Key words, terms, and phrases that the client uses

- Brief description of the client's team members

- Definition of each person's role in the meeting

This short briefing can make the difference between success and failure. It can mean that the client sees a well-coordinated presentation or a bumbling three-ring circus. To steal a line from

> **Rehearse your presentations as a team.**

an old movie, it can mean "never having to say you're sorry" for something that should never have been said. Avoid having to dig yourself out of the holes by making sure you don't dig them in the first place.

Look like a Team of Pros

It's often the little things that make the difference, like common slide backgrounds, consistent facts, and even attire. When they all come together, no one notices. When they don't, it looks like a circus. Your team should pick one style for your graphics, including slides, PowerPoint, and handouts. The marketing department spent millions getting everything just right. Let them help you put the finishing touches on your handouts and presentation graphics too.

As for proper business attire, you don't want to look like security guards at the bank, dressed in identical blue blazers and gray slacks. At the same time, you must make sure you don't have some of your team members dressed casually and the others looking like members of a wedding party. The ultimate goal is for your team to look as if you all arrived from the same place. Even if your factory personnel normally dress differently than your managers in the home office, on presentation day everyone must agree on one style of dress.

You must review your presentations for consistency too. We have all witnessed presentations in which a seller's company president says that he or she has six factories and 12,000 employees and then the director of engineering from the same company says they have seven factories and 13,500 employees. The inconsistency can make the customer begin to wonder if you know what you are doing. They can't imagine how you will ever get their order straight if you can't even remember the fundamental details of your own organization.

> You will be judged by how you look.

A theme is another means of raising your professional image. Have you noticed that conventions that have themes seem to flow smoother? That's because the presenters have a way of linking their programs together, and the audience has a sense of consistency throughout the meeting. A theme for the first example could be "over the top in 12" while the second example might use "beta betters the bottom line." Be sure to tie your theme back to your strategy.

Effective Graphics

If you are not careful, a team presentation can look like a parade of PowerPoint slides in a dark room with various shadowy figures. If that happens, you might just as well have had one presenter do the whole thing. The key is to have the graphics support the points made by the presenter, not the other way around.

> A professional look builds customer confidence.

Ultimately, the presenter needs to outshine the slides so the client can build a rapport with the person, not the screen. This can be done by darkening the area over the screen but leaving the rest of the room well lit. I have often climbed up and taken the bulbs out of the fixture over the screen.

Summary

Customers measure your team by your presentations, and they measure your offering by your team. A customer presentation is more than a sales pitch. It is an opportunity to show the customer that your company has the professionalism to serve them at the high level that they are expecting. Take the time to give your presentation the effort that it deserves.

Appendix A

Troubleshooting Your
Team Selling Process

Infighting, customer complaints, dropped balls, opportunities missed, internal complaints, compensation complaints, and low motivation are the seven most common symptoms of problem teams. The accompanying team problem analysis chart (Figure A-1) lists 31 possible causes of these symptoms. This appendix contains advice for correcting each of these problems.

Reasons Why Sales Teams Fail

Unhealthy Competition

Some companies have spent years building competitive environments that pitted one person against another in the hopes of getting the best out of each one. Improperly focused internal competition can be destructive to teams.

Competition can thrive in team environments if it is channeled properly. Teams can compete against a goal or for prizes and bonuses. They can compete for bragging rights and prestige. It is possible to capture an aggressive and competitive spirit and still gain the advantages of teams.

Figure A-1
Team Problem Analysis Chart

	Infighting	Customer complaints	Dropped balls	Opportunities missed	Internal complaints	Compensation complaints	Low motivation
Unhealthy competition	X	X	X	X	X	X	X
Insufficient team building	X					X	X
Lack of planning	X	X	X	X	X	X	X
Blind faith in teams	X						X
Lack of management support	X			X	X	X	X
Inability to deal with conflict	X				X		X
Lack of protocols	X	X	X	X	X		X
Lack of opportunity for recognition	X				X	X	X
Lack of training	X	X	X	X	X	X	X
Low trust levels	X				X		X
Managers who don't let go				X	X	X	
Lack of cooperation	X	X	X	X	X		X
Lack of accountability		X	X	X	X	X	
Unclear definitions	X			X			X
Changing authority and directions	X		X	X	X		X
Leaders who don't let go	X		X	X	X		X
Not given authority	X				X		X
Do not understand how to use combined abilities				X	X		
Do not have vested interest in outcome				X			X
Do not understand how team works	X			X	X		
Lack of alignment				X	X		
Unclear goals	X			X			
Cookie-cutter approach used				X			X
Unclear roles					X		

Figure A-1 (*Continued*)
Team Problem Analysis Chart

	Infighting	Customer complaints	Dropped balls	Opportunities missed	Internal complaints	Compensation complaints	Low motivation
Improper or insufficient staffing	X	X	X	X	X	X	X
Team leader not doing job					X	X	
Communication breaks down	X	X	X	X			
Team structure too complicated	X		X	X	X		
Micromanaged						X	X
Lack of "face time"	X			X	X		X
Cultural differences	X				X		X

Insufficient Team Building

Given the opportunity, support, and training, teams go through the four stages of organizing, defining, strategizing, and performing, as detailed in Chapter 2. These steps take time. Many companies rush this process and end up with teams stuck in the organizing phase, where constant bickering and complaining characterize their behavior.

To cure these teams, have a qualified team specialist work them through the stages from the beginning.

Lack of Planning

Sales team members who have been operating in a solo manner and are used to "doing" may have a difficult time understanding the need for planning. Where one person can often get by doing what comes up on a given day, only planning and coordination work for teams.

To cure these teams, show them the value of planning and offer a planning skills workshop.

Blind Faith in Teams

If your company is forming sales teams to handle every account, you should review your team policy.

Define the value that teams bring to the sales effort versus the negatives that they produce. You should use teams only when they are the best way to handle the situation.

Lack of Management Support

Building a team culture takes time, understanding, and a commitment by management to the process. Managers who are not supportive will destroy the process through their words and actions.

Managers can start by helping sales teams set realistic sales goals and defining the resources required to achieve them.

Inability to Deal with Conflict

Conflict, not properly dealt with, can tear teams apart.

To resolve conflicts, address the global issues and offer conflict management and communication skills training.

Lack of Protocols

A lack of protocols can cause confusion and misunderstanding. Sales teams require protocols for meetings, communication, brainstorming, and even adding new members in order to function effectively.

Help your teams develop strong protocols to build a foundation for a strong team.

Lack of Opportunity for Recognition

Team members who have been accustomed to being recognized for individual accomplishments may find the team environment unrewarding.

Help your teams learn how to recognize individuals. Remind them that it is only through individual achievement that the team can succeed.

Lack of Training

The difference between a team and a gang is proper training. The lack of training shows up in many ways in sales teams as members invariably have problems with communication, conflicts, meetings, leadership, and time management.

You should plan to invest in training for your teams to reap the true benefits of team work.

Low Trust Levels

Sales teams that lack internal trust are stuck at the defining stage of development.

Outside intervention in the form of a team trainer, who can help them through the process steps they missed, can be effective.

Managers Who Don't Let Go

Managers who have not previously been through the team development process may feel frustrated by the slow progress made in the early stages. If they attempt to intervene, they can confuse their team and often cause the members to abandon their team roles in deference to the manager. Managers who want it done "my way" should not be using teams.

Managers can learn to let go by asking their team how they can best support the members. Managers can set realistic goals and timelines and only check in according to the schedule.

Lack of Cooperation

When sales teams fail to work as teams, ask these questions:

1. Do they know how to work as a team? If not, add training.

2. Does the leader facilitate or direct? Directing leaders need to learn how to build the team from within.

3. Does the team have a common focus? If not, work with this team to clarify their goals.

4. Are members distracted by competing priorities? If so, adjust workloads and priorities as necessary.

Lack of Accountability

Sales teams can be great places for slackers to hide, temporarily.

A good facilitator will ensure that each person is personally responsible for completing specific tasks on specific dates. Project management software can show linked responsibilities in a graphic form.

Unclear Definitions

Sales teams are occasionally developed using a language that can be difficult to decode.

Companies implementing teams should choose their words carefully and define them clearly and universally. When everyone clearly understands the meanings, the potential for confusion is reduced.

Changing Authority and Directions

Frequent changes in management instill doubt in the team and may cause them to unnecessarily slow down to measure the new manager.

When changes are needed, the incoming manager should meet with the team and quickly choose to accept or adjust the goals and plans. Let the team know what you, as the leader, expect and then step back and let them function.

Leaders Who Don't Let Go

Leaders within the sales team often fail to let other team members mature and take on new roles, frustrating the members and hurting performance.

Leaders should ask their teams if they need more autonomy, and teams should be free to express this need, even if they are not asked. If a conflict arises, use a mediator or facilitator to resolve the issue.

Not Given Authority

Having responsibility without authority is a frustrating experience. When teams have clear goals, budgets, and resource plans, they must be free to work within the parameters that have been agreed upon.

Managers may check in periodically to ensure compliance, but the team will only learn to grow when it is allowed to make a few manageable mistakes.

Not Understanding How to Use Their Combined Abilities

New teams are often given good training and then abandoned by well-meaning managers who do not want to be overly controlling. Many of these teams will either abuse or fail to use the authority they have been given.

Managers must check in at regular intervals and help through training, coaching, and team building.

Not Having a Vested Interest in the Team's Goals

Both the team as a whole and the individual members will show poor performance when they can't answer the classic question, What's in it for me?

Managers, team leaders, and team members can help motivate the team through an understanding of the positive outcomes from the given project. Management can help through adjustments in compensation plans, recognition, and other motivators.

Not Understanding How Teams Work

It is often the case that an individual who is underperforming is not able to understand the work that is to be done. The same is true for teams.

Leaders and managers can help by asking the team to present a detailed plan of action detailing the individual tasks to be completed. Coaching and training may be required to assist in areas of low competence.

Lack of Alignment

When any sales team takes action, it should be in support of the goals of the company at large. If not, the team will find itself at odds with others in the company.

The cure is to redefine the team goals so they are in alignment with those of the company. Once in alignment, support for the team should be easier to find.

Unclear Goals

When a team has unclear goals, the members are going in many directions and pulling the team apart.

To assist the team, help them clarify their goals to the point that members can articulate their next five tasks.

Using a Cookie-Cutter Approach

Sales teams must be structured to deal with the specific sales goals for which they were created. Companies should avoid using a one-type-fits-all approach and be flexible in their team creation.

Sales teams that realize they were created or chartered improperly to achieve their objectives should propose changes to management.

Unclear Roles

Roles that are not clear will cause people to revert back to the roles they knew before, destroying the team.

Members of the team should speak up if they are unclear of their new role. Managers may need to help the team members define their new roles.

Improper or Insufficient Staffing

When sales teams are used as a cure for labor cutbacks or cost cutting, they are destined to fail.

Management must either provide proper resources or use a smaller number of teams focused on their biggest opportunities.

The Team Leader Not Doing His or Her Job

A team leader's poor performance can hurt the team's ability to function.

Sales teams should have a protocol for dealing with leaders when there is conflict over responsibilities. These problems should never be ignored, since they will damage the performance of this team and others.

Communication Breaks Down

The larger and more diverse the team is, the greater the chances of a breakdown in communication.

Managers, leaders, or team members may recognize this issue and bring it to the attention of the team and their leadership. Additional training or protocols may be required.

Teaming Structure Is Too Complicated

Many companies feel that teams need to have complicated bureaucracies, fancy names, and rigid structures. Complicated teaming slows action and frustrates everyone.

Streamline your team structure to the minimum required to get the job done. Your teams know where the waste is and can help you restructure!

Micromanagement

The saying "a watched pot never boils" applies to teams as well. If teams don't have the freedom to function, they will stop making decisions.

Managers must learn to watch only the critical issues.

Lack of "Face Time"

Geographically dispersed teams may have a difficult time gelling into a team because of a lack of physical time together. Video conferencing and other technologies are not a good substitute for face-to-face meetings for building rapport and comradery.

Make time for members to meet periodically. If the project is important, it is well worth the investment.

Cultural Differences

In today's dispersed and international work arena, more and more teams are more than a little cross-cultural. A typical team may be made up of members on three or four continents and as many nationalities and customs.

When cultural differences cause a problem on your team, taking time to develop a mutual understanding is the best, and most permanent, cure.

Appendix B

Effective Communication Strategies

For sales teams to be effective, everyone must agree to take 100 percent responsibility for communication, whether they are speaking or listening. In other words, I'm not done explaining until I check with you to ensure you understood what I said, and you must not let me stop until you truly believe you understand. This agreement will end the blame-game and ensure your teams communicate effectively.

Four Steps to Ensure You Convey the Message You Intend to Convey

1. *Give clear explanations.* Recognize and adjust for the knowledge level of the listener.

2. *Encourage active questioning.* Encourage the listener to ask questions, and clarify any areas that were explained poorly.

3. *Confirm feedback.* The speaker must clarify any ambiguities and confirm the assumptions of the listener.

4. *Ensure agreement.*   End the transaction with an agreement by all parties that there appears to be complete understanding.

This is a simple process that maximizes the chance that effective communication will occur by using the 100 percent responsibility rule.

Seven Tips to Help Teams Improve Their Communication Effectiveness

1. *Tell everyone now.*   Whether it is problems, meeting notes, or client changes, the entire team needs to know what is happening as soon as it happens. When many people serve one client, everyone needs to be up-to-speed all the time. It is in each team member's interest to ensure that no one is left out of the loop and that the client always views your company as a well-coordinated team.

2. *Be honest.*   Teams live and die on trust; so honesty is essential to successful team selling. Unfortunately, many people have worked for companies where honesty was only rewarded when the news was good. You must build an environment that also supports those who report bad news.

3. *Be forthright.*   Unfortunately, honesty is not enough to ensure success. If one department fails to disclose everything they know to the others, it will begin to

destroy the organization. Make it clear that it is not sufficient to tell someone the answer to the question he or she asked. Everyone must also disclose the hidden truths that others may never discover if it were not for one person's forthrightness.

4. *Document everything.* Poor notes beat a good memory every time. In team selling, the amount of information handled is large and demands to be written down.

5. *Keep the environment blame-free.* A team can either strive to make the sale work or work to identify the ones who caused it to fail. The atmosphere must be one of mutual support—where anyone who sees a problem is responsible for solving it by bringing it to everyone's attention.

6. *Lead by example.* If you take responsibility for everything you could have fixed, others will do likewise. Communication can be used as a tool for reward and improvement or as a means for criticism and blame. If it is used as the latter, you can be guaranteed that the team members themselves will abandon communication.

7. *Beware of the dangers of e-mail.* E-mail is simply a conversation without the auditory or visual cues that help you accurately interpret intentions, emotions, or other factors. Sales teams need to communicate effectively and must be trained to use tools such as e-mail to clearly convey the intent and attitude of the message.

Three Recommended Communication Protocols[1]

1. *E-mail.* Use for data transfer, information sharing, organizing meetings, and documenting.

2. *Voice-mail.* Use for sharing opinions, operational discussions, context-filled explanations, and single-issue meetings.

3. *Face-to-face.* Use for team building, critical group decisions, sales meetings, strategic decision making, conflict resolution, and brainstorming.

Teams can modify these protocols to fit their specific needs.

Endnotes

Chapter 1

1. "Multi-Functional Teams," *National Account Management Association White Paper No. 1,* 1998, p. 1.

2. Camille Verzal, "Advantages of the Multi-Functional Selling Organization," *Velocity,* Q4 2000, p. 20.

3. Ibid., p. 19.

4. "Multi-Functional Teams," p. 4.

5. Mike Cohn and Jim LoScalzo, "Making Complex Sales Teams Work," *Hewlett-Packard Presentation,* June 1999, p. 8.

6. Monica L. Perry, Craig L. Pearce, and Henry P. Sims Jr., "Empowered Selling Teams: How Shared Leadership Can Contribute to Selling Team Outcomes," *The Journal of Personal Selling & Sales Management* 19, no. 3, summer 1999, p. 2.

7. Rosemary Batt, "Work Organization, Technology, and Performance in Customer Service and Sales," *Industrial & Labor Relations Review,* July 1999, p. 1.

Chapter 4

1. Monica L. Perry, Craig L. Pearch, and Henry P. Sims Jr., "Empowering Selling Teams: How Shared Leadership Can Contribute to Selling Team

Outcomes," *Journal of Personal Selling & Sales Management* 19, no. 3, summer 1999.

2. Deborah L. Duarte and Nancy Tennant Snyder, *Mastering Virtual Teams*, Second Edition (book and CD-ROM), San Francisco: Jossey-Bass, 2001.

3. Perry, Pearch, and Sims, "Empowering Selling Teams."

Chapter 5

1. Eric R. Baron, *Team Selling: Some Thoughts About How to Make It Work*, The Baron Group, Inc., 1994.

Chapter 8

1. "Attendee Survey of Current Trends and Practices in Strategic Account Management," *Strategic Account Management Association*, May 2001, p. 1.

2. Merv Singer and Joanne Gucwa, "Assessing Customer Satisfaction," *The Prepress Bulletin,* www.ipa.org/bulletin/articles/assess_cust_sat.php3.

3. Monica L. Perry, Craig L Pearce, and Henry P. Sims Jr., "Empowered Selling Teams: How Shared Leadership Can Contribute to Selling Team Outcomes," *The Journal of Personal Selling and Sales Management*, summer 1999, p. 14.

4. "Attendee Survey of Current Trends and Practices in Strategic Account Management," *Strategic Account Management Association*, May 2001, p. 15.

5. D. L. Georgenson, "The Problem of Transfer Calls for Partnership," *Training and Development Journal*, 36 (10), 1982, pp. 75–78.

6. P. L. Garavaglia, "How to Ensure Transfer of Training," *Training and Development Journal*, 47 (10), 1993, pp. 63–68.

7. J. M. Werner and A. M. O'Leary, "Augmenting Behavior-Modeling Training: Testing the Effects of Pre- and Post-Training Interventions," *Human Resources Development Quarterly*, 5 (2), 1994, pp. 169–183.

Chapter 9

1. Geoffrey Brewer and Willina Keenan Jr., "Team Selling: Keys to Dividing the Spoils," *Sales and Marketing Management* 146, no. 8, 1994, p. 61.

2. Larry Yu, "Successful Customer-Relationship Management," *MIT Sloan Management Review*, summer 2001.

Chapter 10

1. Neil Rackham, *Major Account Sales Strategy*, New York: McGraw-Hill, 1989, p. 20.

Chapter 12

1. Cornelius Grove, "Cross-Cultural Competencies for Individuals on Global Teams," presentation at 37th Annual SAMA Conference, May 1, 2001.

Appendix B

1. Kathleen Molloy, "Managing Global Teamwork: Cross-Boarder Effectiveness for International Project Teams," *Strategic Account Management Association*, 2001, p. 39.

Index

About the Author

Steve Waterhouse heads the Waterhouse Group. He is a frequent speaker and consultant whose clients include Sun Microsystems, IBM, Xerox, Chrysler, Wyeth-Ayerst, Coca-Cola, United Airlines, Monsanto, and Guidant.